PROBLEMS IN ASIAN CIVILIZATIONS

UNDER THE EDITORIAL DIRECTION OF THE COMMITTEE ON ORIENTAL
STUDIES, COLUMBIA UNIVERSITY

EDITORIAL COMMITTEE: *Wm. Theodore de Bary*, COLUMBIA UNIVERSITY •
Ainslie T. Embree, COLUMBIA UNIVERSITY • *John Meskill*, BARNARD COLLEGE
• *Johanna M. Menzel*, VASSAR COLLEGE • *Arthur Tiedemann*, THE CITY
COLLEGE OF NEW YORK

Other volumes in preparation

PROBLEMS IN ASIAN CIVILIZATIONS

GANDHI

Maker of Modern India?

EDITED WITH AN INTRODUCTION BY

Martin Deming Lewis

SIR GEORGE WILLIAMS UNIVERSITY

D. C. HEATH AND COMPANY · BOSTON

Library of Congress Catalog Card Number 65-17467

Copyright © 1965 by D. C. Heath and Company

BOSTON   ENGLEWOOD   CHICAGO   DALLAS   SAN FRANCISCO   ATLANTA

Printed June 1966

Table of Contents

Introduction

THE history of modern India cannot be understood apart from the career of Mohandas Karamchand Gandhi. From his active entry into India's political life at the end of the First World War to the achievement of Indian independence almost three decades later, his teachings, his activities, and his leadership had profound effects on the course of development in his country. Even after his assassination in 1948, his influence has remained a potent factor in India's evolution.

Yet it is no easy task to evaluate that influence and assess its significance. From one angle of view, he appears as a virtual saint, seeking to bring moral regeneration to India, to her British masters, and even to a troubled world at large. Seen in another light, he seems a shrewd politician, drawing out the latent force of India's millions, guiding and directing it in channels of non-violent direct action toward the goal of Indian freedom from British rule. (The more critical-minded will note that there was a certain ambiguity in this leadership, and that on more than one occasion Gandhi abruptly suspended the nationalist campaign just as it appeared to be within reach of victory.) Finally, in still another dimension of his protean career, Gandhi stands out as a social reformer, attempting to free India from the scars of poverty, caste and class antagonism, untouchability, and conflict between the adherents of Hinduism and Islam.

It is somewhat startling to recall that Gandhi had already reached the age of fifty before he became identified with the thrust of Indian nationalism. Born in 1869,

[1] The term *satyagraha*, meaning "firmness in the truth" or "truth force," was devised by Gandhi

he had gone to England as a young man to study law, and then had spent the middle years of his life in South Africa. It was in South Africa that he had developed his philosophy and technique of *satyagraha*[1] as an instrument for redressing the grievances of the immigrant Indian minority in that country. Only in 1915 did he return permanently to his native India. There, he established an *ashram* or religious colony where he settled with a small band of disciples and co-workers. At first he held back from nationalist activity, and even worked in support of the British war effort. It was not until 1919 that he began to play an influential role in the Indian National Congress.

The Congress itself had been in existence since 1885. For the first two decades it had been led by the so-called "Moderates," westernized Indian intellectuals and professional men for whom the most damning epithet was to say that British rule in India was "un-British" in character. The goals of the Moderates were modest, their following limited, and their activity confined to the adoption of resolutions and the presentation of petitions. Gopal Krishna Gokhale, who died in 1915, was an outstanding representative of this first phase of nationalism.

Early in the twentieth century another

to describe an approach which sought victory not by the forcible *defeat* of the opponent, but by the *conversion* of the opponent through one's own self-suffering. Although Gandhi himself had used the phrase "passive resistance" in the early stages of his movement in South Africa, he later rejected it in favor of *satyagraha*. The movements of "non-violent non-cooperation" and of "civil disobedience" which Gandhi led in India may be considered forms of *satyagraha*; so too were the fasts which he undertook on several occasions for social or political goals.

trend began to make its mark on the Congress, that of the "Extremists" like Bal Gangadhar Tilak (d. 1920), who found their inspiration not in the British system of representative government but in the proud record of India's independent past. The tone of their demands was symbolized by Tilak's ringing phrase, "*Swaraj* [self-rule] is my birth-right, and I will have it!" Related to this development, if not directly allied with it, there also emerged a militant nationalism which resorted to terrorism and revolutionary conspiracies in the cause of Indian freedom.

While the Congress was avowedly secular and national in its aims, it drew its strength primarily from India's majority community, the Hindus. Some Indian Muslims took part in the work of the Congress but more held aloof, or even were repelled by Tilak's aggressive appeal to Hindu tradition. Meanwhile, in 1906, the All-India Muslim League had been formed to give expression to Muslim demands for safeguards against Hindu domination. In the years just before World War I, however, the League and the Congress drew closer, and with the adoption of the "Lucknow Pact" in 1916 they established, temporarily, a common front in their demands for home rule. As yet neither group had attained a mass base of popular support, but the events of the war years served to stimulate nationalist ambitions and to lay the groundwork for a postwar upsurge.

Four events in 1919 and 1920 stirred Indian opinion deeply: (1) the adoption of the Rowlatt Act extending wartime controls on seditious activity; (2) the Amritsar Massacre, when 379 Indians were killed and 1,137 wounded in the course of dispersing a political gathering; (3) the passage of the Government of India Act of 1919 (the Montagu-Chelmsford Reforms), whose terms were a disappointment to nationalists who had expected more substantial political concessions in return for India's loyalty during the war; and, finally, (4) the announcement of the terms of the Treaty of Sèvres dismembering the Ottoman Empire, an action which Indian Muslims regarded as an attack on their religion, since the Turkish sultan was also the caliph or spiritual ruler of Islam.

It was in this situation that Gandhi proposed a campaign of "nonviolent non-cooperation" against the British government. His plan was accepted first by the Khilafat Committee (Muslim leaders who resented the Treaty of Sèvres), and then by the Indian National Congress. The result was the opening of a new phase in the history of Indian nationalism.

The Congress, under Gandhi's influence, soon was transformed from a loosely-organized body of limited membership into a disciplined mass movement. It became a broadly-representative nationalist coalition, uniting sophisticated lawyers, prosperous businessmen, and simple peasants, Western-educated intellectuals, devout Hindus, and nationalist Muslims. Three major campaigns were waged by this coalition, in 1920–22, in 1930–34, and again during the Second World War, to bring pressure on the British for political concessions. The history of these campaigns is outlined in the chronology which follows, and the reader may find it useful to refer to this outline while studying the selections in this volume.

Gandhi's relationship with the Congress is difficult to define in conventional political terms. Though he rejected the title, Gandhi was acclaimed as a *mahatma,* a "great soul." There were periods when he withdrew from active leadership, or even from formal membership in the Congress. Yet for nearly three decades he remained its most prominent single figure, its "permanent super-president," as Jawaharlal Nehru called him in the 1930's.

This is not to say that all Indians were united in support either of Gandhi's leadership or the policies of the Congress. In the early 1920's, the Muslim League was overshadowed by the Khilafat Committee, but the eclipse of the League was only temporary. With the failure of the Khilafat movement[2] it emerged once again as a rival to the Congress, challenging the Congress claim to speak for Muslims as well as Hindus. From the other side, some Hindu nationalists would blame Gandhi for what they felt were unwarranted concessions to Muslim demands. Radical elements within and without the Congress attacked Gandhi's leadership as weak and vacillating. Conversely, the Indian Liberals, heirs of the "Moderates," criticized Gandhi's non-cooperation for obstructing peaceful progress toward the development of self-governing institutions. With all these qualifications, however, the fact remains that the coalition headed by Gandhi and the Congress proved remarkably durable, and the India of today is its handiwork.

In this volume, we are concerned less with the principles of "Gandhism" in the abstract than we are with the specific historical role which he played in the life of his country. The readings in the first section reveal the image of Gandhi that was held by his supporters and followers. Those in the second section illustrate the arguments of some of his critics. The third section presents retrospective attempts at reassessment, while the fourth and final section offers two summary views of Gandhi's impact on the course of development in modern India.

In studying the readings, it may be helpful to keep certain questions in mind. How was it that Gandhi came so suddenly to leadership in the Congress, after years spent away from his homeland? What turned him from a supporter of British rule into a champion of the nationalist cause? How effective was his technique of *satyagraha* as an instrument for the winning of independence? How effective was Gandhi's generalship? In questions of social reform, what answers did Gandhi offer for India's problems, and what changes did they bring in the texture of Indian life? How influential were his efforts on behalf of the untouchables? What was the significance of his approach to India's economic problems? What effect did his leadership have on the development of the Hindu-Muslim communal issue? Must he bear some share of responsibility for the partition of India which he had so steadfastly opposed? All of these questions, and more, must be posed in attempting an estimate of Gandhi's unique role in the making of modern India.

[2] While the Khilafat movement in India failed to win modification of the Treaty of Sèvres, Turkey's own nationalists under Kemal Atatürk did succeed in preventing the implementation of those parts of the treaty which would have dismembered Turkey proper (Anatolia), and they won recognition of their stand by the Treaty of Lausanne in 1923. However, the Turkish revolutionaries then proceeded in 1924 to exile the sultan and decree the abolition of the caliphate.

[NOTE: Footnotes generally have been omitted from the selections, except where they are necessary for clarity or where they make a substantial contribution to the author's argument.]

Chronology

1869 October 2. Mohandas Karamchand Gandhi born at Porbandar, India.

1893–1914 Gandhi in South Africa; develops *satyagraha* technique in campaigns to defend rights of Indian immigrants in South Africa.

1915 Gandhi returns permanently to India.

1919 March 18. Rowlatt Act to control seditious activity becomes law.
April 6. *Hartal* (day of suspension of business) called by Gandhi to protest Rowlatt Act; *Satyagraha Sabha* organized by him to continue protest.
April 13. Amritsar Massacre in the Panjab.
April 18. Gandhi suspends *satyagraha* because of outbreaks of violence.
December. Montagu-Chelmsford Reforms become law; Gandhi urges their acceptance by Indian National Congress.

1920 May 15. Terms of Treaty of Sèvres announced (World War I peace treaty with Turkey which dismembered the Ottoman Empire).
May 28. Report of Hunter Committee on Amritsar Massacre published.
June 2. Khilafat Committee accepts Gandhi's proposal for non-cooperation with the government to protest terms of the Treaty of Sèvres; all-India *hartal* called for August 1 to support Khilafat movement demands.
September. Special session of Indian National Congress at Calcutta adopts program of "progressive nonviolent non-cooperation" to secure redress for the Khilafat and the Panjab wrongs, and the establishment of *swaraj*. Decision ratified by regular session of Congress at Nagpur in December.

1921 Progressive implementation of non-cooperation; burning of foreign cloth, picketing of liquor shops, etc.; boycott of Prince of Wales' visit to India in November. Widespread arrests of Congress workers and leaders, reaching a peak in December 1921 and January 1922.

1922 February 1. Gandhi announces intention of calling for mass civil disobedience in Bardoli subdivision, Bombay Presidency (population 87,000).
February 5. Outbreak of violence at village of Chauri Chaura, United Provinces.
February 12. Gandhi and Congress Working Committee at Bardoli call off plans for civil disobedience, citing violence at Chauri Chaura.
March 10. Gandhi arrested; tried and imprisoned until January 12, 1924.

1924–1927 Gandhi holds aloof from political activity, devotes himself to "constructive programme" of Hindu-Muslim amity, removal of untouchability, and popularization of *khadi* (homespun).

1928 Successful *satyagraha* campaign against tax increase in Bardoli subdivision. Boycott of Simon Commission investigating workings of 1919 Reforms.
December. Congress session at Calcutta accepts Nehru Report proposing dominion-status constitution, warns that British failure to accept proposal within one year will bring demand for complete independence, campaign of nonviolent non-cooperation.

1929 October 31. Declaration by viceroy, Lord Irwin: (a) dominion status will be "the natural issue of India's constitutional progress"; (b) a Round Table Conference of British and Indian leaders will be called to meet in London.
December. Congress session at Lahore rejects Round Table Conference, declares for complete independence, authorizes civil disobedience campaign.

1930   March 12–April 6. Gandhi leads 78 disciples on "salt march" to sea at Dandi.
        May 5. Gandhi arrested, imprisoned without trial. Mass arrests of *satyagrahis*.
        November 12–January 19, 1931. First session of Round Table Conference meets at
        London; Indian National Congress is not represented.

1931   January 26. Gandhi and other Congress leaders released from prison.
        March 5. Gandhi-Irwin Pact: Congress suspends civil disobedience, agrees to attend
        second session of Round Table Conference.
        September 7–December 1. Second session of Round Table Conference; Gandhi at-
        tends as sole representative of Congress, fails to reach agreement.

1932   January 4. Gandhi arrested, imprisoned without trial. Civil disobedience resumed.
        Mass arrests.
        August 17. Prime Minister MacDonald's "Communal Award" giving separate elec-
        torate to untouchables.
        September 20. Gandhi, in jail, begins fast "unto death" against Communal Award.
        September 26. Gandhi ends fast after "Poona Pact" with untouchable leaders is ac-
        cepted by MacDonald; untouchables to get reserved seats but no separate electorate.

1933   May 9. Government releases Gandhi from prison as he begins fast for self-purification.
        Congress suspends mass civil disobedience, but authorizes *satyagraha* by individuals.

1934   May 20. Congress suspends all civil disobedience except for that which may be offered
        by Gandhi personally.
        October. Gandhi retires from formal membership in Indian National Congress.

1934–1939   Gandhi holds aloof from overt political activity, devotes himself to "constructive
        programme."

1937   Congress contests elections under Government of India Act of 1935, forms ministries
        and takes office in seven provinces.

1939   September 3. Great Britain declares war on Germany after invasion of Poland; viceroy
        declares that India is also at war.
        November 8. Congress ministries resign after British government refuses action on
        Congress demand for immediate independence.

1940   March. All-India Muslim League adopts demand for creation of separate independent
        Muslim state of Pakistan.
        October 17. Congress launches campaign of individual *satyagraha;* continues through
        1941.

1942   March 22–April 12. Cripps Mission fails to resolve deadlock between Congress and
        British government.
        August 8. Congress adopts "Quit India" resolution, calls for "mass struggle on non-
        violent lines" under slogan "Do or Die." Gandhi and other Congress leaders arrested
        August 9. Gandhi released May 6, 1944; other major leaders released June 14, 1945.

1945   August 14. World War II ends with Japanese surrender.

1946–1947   Negotiations between British government, Indian National Congress, and All-
        India Muslim League, culminating in agreement on partition of India despite Gandhi's
        opposition.

1947   August 15. Independence of India and Pakistan.

1948   January 30. Gandhi assassinated by Hindu fanatic.

The Conflict of Opinion

"Then Gandhi came. He was like a powerful current of fresh air that made us stretch ourselves and take deep breaths, like a beam of light that pierced the darkness and removed the scales from our eyes, like a whirlwind that upset many things but most of all the working of people's minds. He did not descend from the top; he seemed to emerge from the millions of India, speaking their language and incessantly drawing attention to them and their appalling condition. Get off the backs of these peasants and workers, he told us, all you who live by their exploitation; get rid of the system that produces this poverty and misery."

— JAWAHARLAL NEHRU

"That he diverted the energy and direction of Indian politics from Europe to India was Gandhiji's greatest achievement. Instead of attempting an Ersatz Europe, he sought to build up a genuine India. . . . Gandhiji did not quarrel with facts. He sought to use them for his own purposes. He accepted the fatalism and passivity of the Indian people but found for them a new political function. Instead of an aggressive and militant struggle, he built up a movement of non-cooperation in which passivity and endurance were turned into sources of strength and energy."

— HUMAYUN KABIR

"[Gandhi] was the most subtle and experienced politician of the older group . . . the ascetic defender of property in the name of the most religious and idealist principles of humility and love of poverty . . . the prophet who by his personal saintliness and selflessness could unlock the door to the hearts of the masses where the moderate bourgeois leaders could not hope for a hearing — and the best guarantee of the shipwreck of any mass movement which had the blessing of his association. This Jonah of revolution, this general of unbroken disasters was the mascot of the bourgeoisie in each wave of the developing Indian struggle."

— RAJANI PALME DUTT

"To the Untouchables, Hinduism is a veritable chamber of horrors. The sanctity and infallibility of the Vedas, Smritis and Shastras, the iron law of caste, the heartless law of *karma* and the senseless law of status by birth . . . are to be found intact and untarnished in the bosom of Gandhism."

— B. R. AMBEDKAR

"If we delineate the political life of Gandhi with strict adherence to truth, it will, I believe, be patent to all that Gandhi was lacking in both political wisdom and political strategy . . . and far from being infallible, committed serious blunders, one after another, in pursuit of some Utopian ideals and methods which had no basis in reality. . . . The current estimate of the degree or extent of his success bears no relation to actual facts."

— R. C. MAJUMDAR

"Gandhi had a fundamental, moral objection to the demand for independence outside the Empire. He considered such a demand to be unrighteous — indicating a want of faith in God and in human nature. . . . Nonviolent non-cooperation, Gandhi never ceased to reiterate, was not a program for the seizure of power, but for the conversion of Englishmen. . . . There can be little doubt that but for Gandhi's determined opposition the Congress — and even the Muslim League — would have gone over to secession and republicanism in 1920–21."

— S. R. Mehrotra

"When I characterised Gandhi as the ideological representative of the bourgeoisie, I did not at all ascribe to him any motive of protecting the interests of the bourgeoisie. It is a misfortune of every human being that history's verdict of what he or she does is different from what he or she thinks he or she does. Mahatma Gandhi may have honestly believed that he was safeguarding the interests of the entire nation and not of a particular class or community. The point is: What were the actual results of this practical activity?"

— E. M. S. Namboodiripad

"In his own major purpose Gandhi may be considered to have failed. His aim was the religious regeneration of India and Indians. As success for nationalism became step by step more likely, the politicians slipped out more and more from his control. They had no faith in the ultimate value of his religious purpose, as he had none in the ultimate worth of any purely secular end. He had said that he made a religious use of politics; many a politician of the time, if frank, would have admitted that he, in his turn, was making a political use of religion. . . . Though Gandhi abhorred Hindu-Muslim communalism and partition, he nevertheless contributed to them. He could not in his time have become the political leader of the majority group in India, fortified by mass support, without being religious, he could not be religious without being Hindu. He could not be Hindu without being suspect to the Muslim community."

— W. Norman Brown

"Some of the teachings of Gandhiji have passed into the general traditions of India, but strangely enough not those to which he attached the greatest importance, *ahimsa, satyagraha,* voluntary poverty, etc. . . . In many cases, like social reform, betterment of women, Gandhi's influence has given only an additional impetus to an already growing movement 100 years old. In others, like the abolition of untouchability, the widening of Hinduism to include in it all the classes which had been considered *avarnas* — or outside the caste system — his teaching, practice and influence was the predominant factor. All in all, the Mahatma is justly acclaimed the Father of the Nation, though with the growth of an industrialized society, it is difficult to be certain whether his influence will continue."

— K. M. Panikkar

GANDHI: FATHER OF THE NATION

On Gandhi

JAWAHARLAL NEHRU

As Gandhi's foremost follower, Jawaharlal Nehru (1889–1964) was uniquely qualified to tell of his impact on India. In Nehru's writings extensive accounts will be found of the campaigns which Gandhi led in the 1920's and 1930's. The excerpts presented here, however, give his judgment of the man and his place in the development of the nationalist movement. They are drawn from four different works: Nehru's *Autobiography* (1936; published in the United States as *Toward Freedom* in 1941); *Glimpses of World History* (1942); *The Discovery of India* (1946); and *India and the World* (1936).

My first meeting with Gandhiji[1] was about the time of the Lucknow [session of the Indian National] Congress during Christmas, 1916. All of us admired him for his heroic fight in South Africa, but he seemed very distant and different and unpolitical to many of us young men. He refused to take part in Congress or national politics then and confined himself to the South African Indian question. Soon afterward his adventures and victory in Champaran, on behalf of the tenants of the planters, filled us with enthusiasm. We saw that he was prepared to apply his methods in India also, and they promised success.

* * *

India waited after the war; resentful, rather aggressive, not very hopeful, but still expectant. Within a few months, the first fruits of the new British policy, so eagerly waited for, appeared in the shape of a proposal to pass special laws to control the revolutionary movement. Instead of more freedom, there was to be more repression. These bills were based on the report of a committee and were known as the Rowlatt Bills. But very soon they were called the "Black Bills" all over the country, and were denounced everywhere and by every Indian, including even the most moderate. They gave great powers to the government and the police to arrest, keep in prison without trial, or to have a secret trial of any person they disapproved of or suspected. A famous description of these bills at the time

[1] I have referred to Mr. Gandhi or Mahatma Gandhi as "Gandhiji," as he himself preferred this to the addition of *Mahatma* to his name. *Ji* is one of the commonest additions to a name in India, being applied indiscriminately to all kinds of people and to men, women, boys, girls, and children. It conveys an idea of respect, something equivalent to Mr., Mrs., or Miss. Hindustani is rich in courtly phrases and prefixes and suffixes to names and honorific titles. *Ji* is the simplest of these and the least formal of them, though perfectly correct.

was: *na vakīl, na appeal, na dalīl*.[2] As the outcry against the bills gained volume, a new factor appeared, a little cloud on the political horizon which grew and spread rapidly till it covered the Indian sky.

This new factor was Mohandas Karamchand Gandhi. He had returned to India from South Africa during wartime and settled down with his colony in an *ashram* in Sabarmati. He had kept away from politics. He had even helped the government in recruiting men for the war. He was, of course, very well known in India since his *satyagraha* struggle in South Africa. In 1917 he had championed with success the miserable downtrodden tenants of the European planters in the Champaran district of Bihar. Later he had stood up for the peasantry of Kaira in Gujrat. Early in 1919 he was very ill. He had barely recovered from it when the Rowlatt Bill agitation filled the country. He also joined his voice to the universal outcry.

But this voice was somehow different from the others. It was quiet and low, and yet it could be heard above the shouting of the multitude; it was soft and gentle, and yet there seemed to be steel hidden away somewhere in it; it was courteous and full of appeal, and yet there was something grim and frightening in it; every word used was full of meaning and seemed to carry a deadly earnestness. Behind the language of peace and friendship there was power and the quivering shadow of action and a determination not to submit to a wrong. We are familiar with that voice now; we have heard it often enough during the last fourteen years. But it was new to us in February and March 1919; we did not quite know what to make of it, but we were thrilled. This was something very different from our noisy politics of condemnation and nothing else, long speeches always ending in the same futile and ineffective resolutions of protest which nobody took very seriously. This was the politics of action, not of talk.

Mahatma Gandhi organized a *Satyagraha Sabha* [Satyagraha League] of those who were prepared to break chosen laws and thus court imprisonment. This was quite a novel idea then, and many of us were excited but many shrank back. Today it is the most commonplace of occurrences, and for most of us it has become a fixed and regular part of our lives!

As usual with him, Gandhi sent a courteous appeal and warning to the Viceroy. When he saw that the British government were determined to pass the law in spite of the opposition of a united India, he called for an all-India day of mourning, a *hartāl*, a stoppage of business, and meetings on the first Sunday after the Bills became law. This was to inaugurate the *satyagraha* movement, and so Sunday. April 6. 1919, was observed as the Satyagraha Day all over the country, in town and village. It was the first all-India demonstration of the kind, and it was a wonderfully impressive one, in which all kinds of people and communities joined. Those of us who had worked for this *hartāl* were amazed at its success. It had been possible for us to approach only a limited number of people in the cities. But a new spirit was in the air, and somehow the message managed to reach the remotest villages of our huge country. For the first time the villager as well as the town worker took part in a political demonstration on a mass scale.

*   *   *

Events marched rapidly after that Satyagraha Day on April 6. There was trouble in Amritsar on April 10. when an unarmed and bareheaded crowd, mourning for the arrest of its leaders, Drs. Kitchlew and Satyapal, was shot at by the military and many were killed; it thereupon took its mad revenge by killing five or six innocent Englishmen, sitting in their offices, and burning their bank buildings. And then a curtain seemed to drop on the Punjab. It was cut off from the rest of India by a rigid censorship; hardly any news came, and it was very difficult for people to enter or leave

[2] I.e., no lawyer, no appeal, no document. [Editor's note]

the province. There was martial law there, and the agony of this continued for many months. Slowly, after weeks and months of agonized suspense, the curtain lifted and the horrible truth was known. . . .

All the world knows of the massacre that took place on April 13 in the Jallianwala Bagh in Amritsar, when thousands fell dead and wounded, in that trap of death from which there was no escape. The very word "Amritsar" has become a synonym for massacre.

* * *

That year, in December 1919, by a curious coincidence, the Congress was held in Amritsar. No great decision was arrived at by this Congress because the result of the inquiries was awaited, but it was evident that the Congress had changed. There was now a mass character about it and a new, and for some of the old Congressmen a disturbing, vitality. There was Lokamanya[3] Tilak, uncompromising as ever, attending his last Congress, for he was to die before the next one was held. There was Gandhi, popular with the crowd, and just beginning his long period of domination over the Congress and Indian politics. There came also to the Congress, straight from prison, many leaders who had been involved in monstrous conspiracy cases during the martial-law days and sentenced to long terms of imprisonment, but were now amnestied, and the famous Ali brothers[4] just released after many years' detention.

The next year the Congress took the plunge, and adopted Gandhi's program of non-cooperation. A special session in Calcutta adopted this [in September, 1920], and later the annual session in Nagpur [in December] confirmed it. The method of struggle was a perfectly peaceful one, non-violent as it was called, and its basis was a refusal to help the government in its administration and exploitation of India. To

begin with there were to be a number of boycotts—of titles given by the foreign government, of official functions and the like, of law-courts by both lawyers and litigants, of official schools and colleges, and of the new councils under the Montagu-Chelmsford reforms.[5] Later the boycotts were to extend to the civil and military services and the payment of taxes. On the constructive side stress was laid on hand spinning and *khaddar*,[6] and on arbitration courts to take the place of the law-courts. Two other most important planks were Hindu-Muslim unity and the removal of untouchability among the Hindus.

The Congress also changed its constitution and became a body capable of action, and at the same time it laid itself out for a mass membership.

Now, this program was a totally different thing from what the Congress had so far been doing; indeed, it was quite a novel thing in the world, for the *satyagraha* in South Africa had been very limited in its scope. It meant immediate and heavy sacrifices for some people, like the lawyers, who were called upon to give up their practices, and the students, who were asked to boycott the government colleges. It was difficult to judge it, as there were no standards of comparison. It is not surprising that the old and experienced Congress leaders hesitated and were filled with doubt. The greatest of them, Lokamanya Tilak, had died a little before this. Of the other prominent Congress leaders only one, Motilal Nehru, supported Gandhi in the early stages. But there was no doubting the temper of the average Congressman, or the man in the street, or the masses. Gandhi

[3] "Saviour of the People." [Editor's note]
[4] Muhammad Ali and Shaukat Ali, Muslim nationalist leaders who had been interned by the British during World War I. [Editor's note]
[5] The Montagu-Chelmsford Reforms, enacted by the British parliament in 1919, had established legislative councils with limited authority at both the central and provincial level. A majority of the membership of the councils was to be chosen by elections held on the basis of a restricted franchise. The first election under the Act, held in 1920, was boycotted by the Indian National Congress as part of the program of non-cooperation. [Editor's note]
[6] *Khaddar* or *khadi*: hand-spun and woven cloth. [Editor's note]

carried them off their feet, almost hyp-
notized them, and with loud shouts of *Mahatma Gandhi ki jai* ["long live Mahatma
Gandhi"], they showed their approval of
the new gospel of nonviolent non-cooperation. The Muslims were as enthusiastic
about it as the others. Indeed, the *Khilafat*
Committee, under the leadership of the Ali
brothers, had adopted the program even before the Congress did so. Soon the mass enthusiasm and the early successes of the
movement brought most of the old Congress leaders into it.

*   *   *

The growth of nationalism turned people's minds to the necessity for political
freedom. Freedom was necessary not only
because it was degrading to be dependent
and enslaved, not only because, as Tilak
had put it, it was our birthright and we
must have it, but also to lessen the burden
of poverty from our people. How was freedom to be obtained? Obviously, we were
not going to get it by remaining quiet and
waiting for it. It was equally clear that
methods of mere protest and begging,
which the Congress had so far followed
with more or less vehemence, were not only
undignified for a people, but were also
futile and ineffective. Never in history had
such methods succeeded or induced a ruling or privileged class to part with power.
History, indeed, showed us that peoples
and classes who were enslaved had won
their freedom through violent rebellion and
insurrection.

Armed rebellion seemed out of the question for the Indian people. We were dis-
armed, and most of us did not even know
the use of arms. Besides, in a contest of
violence, the organized power of the British
government, or any state, was far greater
than anything that could be raised against
it. Armies might mutiny, but unarmed people could not rebel and face armed forces.
Individual terrorism, on the other hand, the
killing by bomb or pistol of individual of-
ficers, was a bankrupt's creed. It was de-
moralizing for the people, and it was ri-

diculous to think that it could shake a powerfully organized government, however
much it might frighten individuals.

*   *   *

So all these avenues led nowhere, and
there seemed to be no way out of the in-
tolerable conditions of a degrading servi-
tude. People who were at all sensitive felt
terribly depressed and helpless. This was
the moment when Gandhi put forward his
program of non-cooperation. Like Sinn
Fein in Ireland, it taught us to rely on ourselves and build up our own strength, and
it was obviously a very effective method of
bringing pressure on the government. The
government rested very largely on the cooperation, willing or unwilling, of Indians
themselves, and if this cooperation were
withdrawn and the boycotts practiced, it
was quite possible, in theory, to bring down
the whole structure of government. Even
if the non-cooperation did not go so far,
there was no doubt that it could exert tremendous pressure on the government, and
at the same time increase the strength of
the people. It was to be perfectly peaceful,
and yet it was not mere non-resistance. *Satyagraha* was a definite, though nonviolent,
form of resistance to what was considered
wrong. It was, in effect, a peaceful rebellion, a most civilized form of warfare, and
yet dangerous to the stability of the state.
It was an effective way of getting the
masses to function, and it seemed to fit in
with the peculiar genius of the Indian people. It put us on our best behavior and
seemed to put the adversary in the wrong.
It made us shed the fear that crushed us,
and we began to look people in the face
as we had never done before, and to speak
out our minds fully and frankly. A great
weight seemed to be lifted from our minds,
and this new freedom of speech and action
filled us with confidence and strength. And,
finally, the method of peace prevented to
a large extent the growth of those terribly
bitter racial and national hatreds which
had always so far accompanied such strug-

gles, and thus made the ultimate settlement easier.

It is not surprising, therefore, that this program of non-cooperation, coupled with the remarkable personality of Gandhi, caught the imagination of the country and filled it with hope. It spread, and at its approach the old demoralization vanished. The new Congress attracted most of the vital elements in the country and grew in power and prestige.

*   *   *

Not for a few years of excitement and agony and suspense, but for long generations our people had offered their "blood, toil, sweat and tears." And this process had eaten its way deep into the body and soul of India, poisoning every aspect of our corporate life, like that fell disease which consumes the tissues of the lungs and kills slowly but inevitably. Sometimes we thought that some swifter and more obvious process, resembling cholera or the bubonic plague, would have been better. But that was a passing thought, for adventurism leads nowhere, and the quack treatment of deep-seated diseases does not yield results.

And then Gandhi came. He was like a powerful current of fresh air that made us stretch ourselves and take deep breaths, like a beam of light that pierced the darkness and removed the scales from our eyes, like a whirlwind that upset many things but most of all the working of people's minds. He did not descend from the top; he seemed to emerge from the millions of India, speaking their language and incessantly drawing attention to them and their appalling condition. Get off the backs of these peasants and workers, he told us, all you who live by their exploitation; get rid of the system that produces this poverty and misery.

Political freedom took new shape then and acquired a new content. Much that he said we only partially accepted or sometimes did not accept at all. But all this was secondary. The essence of his teaching was fearlessness and truth and action allied to these, always keeping the welfare of the masses in view. The greatest gift for an individual or a nation, so we had been told in our ancient books, was *abhaya*, fearlessness, not merely bodily courage but the absence of fear from the mind. Chanakya and Yagnavalka had said, at the dawn of our history, that it was the function of the leaders of a people to make them fearless. But the dominant impulse in India under British rule was that of fear, pervasive, oppressing, strangling fear; fear of the army, the police, the widespread secret service; fear of the official class; fear of laws meant to suppress, and of prison; fear of the landlord's agent; fear of the moneylender; fear of unemployment and starvation, which were always on the threshold. It was against this all-pervading fear that Gandhi's quiet and determined voice was raised: Be not afraid.

Was it so simple as all that? Not quite. And yet fear builds its phantoms which are more fearsome than reality itself, and reality when calmly analyzed and its consequences willingly accepted loses much of its terror.

So, suddenly as it were, that black pall of fear was lifted from the people's shoulders, not wholly, of course, but to an amazing degree. As fear is close companion to falsehood, so truth follows fearlessness. The Indian people did not become much more truthful than they were, nor did they change their essential nature overnight; nevertheless a sea change was visible as the need for falsehood and furtive behavior lessened. It was a psychological change, almost as if some expert in psychoanalytical method had probed deep into the patient's past, found out the origins of his complexes, exposed them to his view, and thus rid him of that burden.

*   *   *

The older leaders of the Congress, nurtured in a different and more quiescent tradition, did not take easily to these new ways and were disturbed by the upsurge of the masses. Yet so powerful was the wave of feeling and sentiment that swept through the country that some of that intoxication filled them also. A very few fell away, and among them was Mr. M. A. Jinnah.[7] He left the Congress not because of any difference of opinion on the Hindu-Muslim question but because he could not adapt himself to the new and more advanced ideology, and even more because he disliked the crowds of ill-dressed people, talking in Hindustani, who filled the Congress. His idea of politics was of a superior variety, more suited to the legislative chamber or to a committee room. For some years he felt completely out of the picture and even decided to leave India for good. He settled down in England and spent several years there.

It is said, and I think with truth, that the Indian habit of mind is essentially one of quietism. Perhaps old races develop that attitude to life; a long tradition of philosophy also leads to it. And yet Gandhi, a typical product of India, represents the very antithesis of quietism. He has been a demon of energy and action, a hustler, and a man who not only drives himself but drives others. He has done more than anyone I know to fight and change the pietism of the Indian people.

He sent us to the villages, and the countryside hummed with the activity of innumerable messengers of the new gospel of action. The peasant was shaken up and he began to emerge from his quiescent shell. The effect on us was different but equally far-reaching, for we saw, for the first time as it were, the villager in the intimacy of his mud hut and with the stark shadow of hunger always pursuing him. We learned our Indian economics more from these visits than from books and learned discourses. The emotional experience we had already undergone was emphasized and confirmed, and henceforward there could be no going back for us to our old life or our old standards, howsoever much our views might change subsequently.

Gandhi held strong views on economic, social, and other matters. He did not try to impose all of these on the Congress, though he continued to develop his ideas, and sometimes in the process varied them, through his writings. But some he tried to push into the Congress. He proceeded cautiously, for he wanted to carry the people with him. Sometimes he went too far for the Congress and had to retrace his steps. Not many accepted his views in their entirety; some disagreed with that fundamental outlook. But many accepted them in the modified form in which they came to the Congress as being suited to the circumstances then existing. In two respects the background of his thoughts had a vague but considerable influence: the fundamental test of everything was how far it benefited the masses, and the means were always important and could not be ignored even though the end in view was right, for the means governed the end and varied it.

Gandhi was essentially a man of religion, a Hindu to the innermost depths of his being, and yet his conception of religion had nothing to do with any dogma or custom or ritual.[8] It was basically concerned with his firm belief in the moral law, which he calls the Law of Truth or Love. Truth and nonviolence appear to him to be the same thing or different aspects of one and the same thing, and he uses these words almost interchangeably.

[7] The Muslim leader Muhammad Ali Jinnah (1876–1948) had been a prominent figure in the Congress for more than a decade. After leaving the Congress in 1920 he became active in the All-India Muslim League and was chosen its permanent president in 1934. From 1940 onward, Jinnah was the foremost spokesman for the idea of partitioning India and creating a separate Muslim state of Pakistan. [Editor's note]

[8] Gandhi told the Federation of International Fellowships in January 1928 that "after long study and experience I have come to these conclusions, that: (1) all religions are true, (2) all religions have some error in them, (3) all religions are almost as dear to me as my own Hinduism. My veneration for other faiths is the same as for my own faith. Consequently, the thought of conversion is impossible. . . . Our prayer for others ought never to be: 'God! give them the light thou has given to me!' but: 'Give them all the light and truth they need for their highest development!' "

Claiming to understand the spirit of Hinduism, he rejects every text or practice which does not fit in with his idealist interpretation of what it should be, calling it an interpolation or a subsequent accretion. "I decline to be a slave," he has said, "to precedents or practice I cannot understand or defend on a moral basis." And so in practice he is singularly free to take the path of his choice, to change and adapt himself, to develop his philosophy of life and action, subject only to the overriding consideration of the moral law as he conceives this to be. Whether that philosophy is right or wrong may be argued, but he insists on applying the same fundamental yardstick to everything, and himself specially in politics, as in other aspects of life, this creates difficulties for the average person, and often misunderstanding. But no difficulty makes him swerve from the straight line of his choosing, though within limits he is continually adapting himself to a changing situation. Every reform that he suggests, every advice that he gives to others, he straightway applies to himself. He is always beginning with himself, and his words and actions fit into each other like a glove on a hand. And so, whatever happens, he never loses his integrity and there is always an organic completeness about his life and work. Even in his apparent failures he has seemed to grow in stature.

What was his idea of India which he was setting out to mold according to his own wishes and ideals?

I shall work for an India in which the poorest shall feel that it is their country, in whose making they have an effective voice, an India in which there shall be no high class and low class of people, an India in which all communities shall live in perfect harmony. . . . There can be no room in such an India for the curse of untouchability or the curse of intoxicating drinks and drugs. . . . Women who will enjoy the same rights as men. . . . This is the India of my dreams.

Proud of his Hindu inheritance as he was, he tried to give to Hinduism a kind of universal attire and included all religions within the fold of truth. He refused to narrow his cultural inheritance. "Indian culture," he wrote, "is neither Hindu, Islamic nor any other, wholly. It is a fusion of all." Again he said:

I want the culture of all lands to be blown about my house as freely as possible. But I refuse to be blown off my feet by any. I refuse to live in other people's houses as an interloper, a beggar or a slave.

Influenced by modern thought currents, he never let go of his roots and clung to them tenaciously.

And so he set about to restore the spiritual unity of the people and to break the barrier between the small westernized group at the top and the masses, to discover the living elements in the old roots and to build upon them, to waken these masses out of their stupor and static condition and make them dynamic. . . .

It is not surprising that this astonishingly vital man, full of self-confidence and an unusual kind of power, standing for equality and freedom for each individual, but measuring all this in terms of the poorest, fascinated the masses of India and attracted them like a magnet. He seemed to them to link up the past with the future and to make the dismal present appear just as a steppingstone to that future of life and hope. And not the masses only, but intellectuals, and others also, though their minds were often troubled and confused and the change-over for them from the habits of lifetimes was more difficult. Thus he effected a vast psychological revolution not only among those who followed his lead but also among his opponents and those many neutrals who could not make up their minds what to think and what to do.

Congress was dominated by Gandhi, and yet it was a peculiar domination, for the Congress was an active, rebellious, many-sided organization, full of variety of opinion, and not easily led this way or that.

Often Gandhi toned down his position to meet the wishes of others; sometimes he accepted even an adverse decision. On some vital matters for him he was adamant, and on more than one occasion there came a break between him and the Congress. But always he was the symbol of India's independence and militant nationalism, the unyielding opponent of all those who sought to enslave her, and it was as such a symbol that people gathered to him and accepted his lead, even though they disagreed with him on other matters. They did not always accept that lead when there was no active struggle going on, but when the struggle was inevitable, that symbol became all-important and everything else was secondary.

*   *   *

It should be remembered that the nationalist movement in India, like all nationalist movements, was essentially a bourgeois movement. It represented the natural historical stage of development, and to consider or to criticize it as a working-class movement is wrong. Gandhi represented that movement and the Indian masses in relation to that movement to a supreme degree, and he became the voice of the Indian people to that extent. He functioned inevitably within the orbit of nationalist ideology, but the dominating passion that consumed him was a desire to raise the masses. In this respect he was always ahead of the nationalist movement, and he gradually made it, within the limits of its own ideology, turn in this direction. Economic events in India and the world powerfully pushed Indian nationalism toward vital social changes, and today it hovers, somewhat undecided, on the brink of a new social ideology.

But the main contribution of Gandhi to India and the Indian masses has been through the powerful movements which he launched through the National Congress. Through nation-wide action he sought to mold the millions, and largely succeeded in doing so, and changing them from a demoralized, timid, and hopeless mass, bullied and crushed by every dominant interest, and incapable of resistance, into a people with self-respect and self-reliance, resisting tyranny, and capable of united action and sacrifice for a larger cause. He made them think of political and economic issues, and every village and every bazaar hummed with argument and debate on the new ideas and hopes that filled the people. That was an amazing psychological change. The time was ripe for it, of course, and circumstances and world conditions worked for this change. But a great leader is necessary to take advantage of circumstances and conditions. Gandhi was that leader, and he released many of the bonds that imprisoned and disabled our minds, and none of us who experienced it can ever forget that great feeling of release and exhilaration that came over the Indian people. Gandhi has played a revolutionary role in India of the greatest importance because he knew how to make the most of the objective conditions and could reach the heart of the masses; while groups with a more advanced ideology functioned largely in the air because they did not fit in with those conditions and could therefore not evoke any substantial response from the masses. . . .

It is perfectly true that Gandhi, functioning in the nationalist plane, does not think in terms of the conflict of classes, and tries to compose their differences. But the action he has indulged in and taught the people has inevitably raised mass consciousness tremendously and made social issues vital. And his insistence on the raising of the masses at the cost, wherever necessary, of vested interests has given a strong orientation to the national movement in favor of the masses. . . .

The Father of the Nation

D. S. SARMA

This interpretation, written from the vantage point of the success of the nationalist movement in winning independence, lays stress on Gandhi's place in the Hindu religious tradition. D. S. Sarma, the retired Principal of Vivekananda College in Madras, is the author of more than ten volumes on Hinduism, including A Primer of Hinduism, The Gandhi Sutras, Lectures and Essays on the Bhagavat Gita, and The Renaissance of Hinduism, as well as The Father of the Nation: The Life and Teachings of Mahatma Gandhi (1956) from which the following selection is drawn.

MAHATMA Gandhi has been rightly described as the Father of our Nation. He was the architect of India's freedom. He did far more than anyone had ever done before in Indian history to weld together, into one compact whole, the various sections of India's population — Hindus and Muslims, caste Hindus and outcastes, and town-dwellers and the village folk. Moreover in the long history of our country no man has touched our national life at so many points or so intensely as he has done. We have had great religious teachers, great law-givers and great statesmen, but no single character in the past has influenced our people in such a variety of ways as Gandhiji has done. His influence has been felt in the political sphere, in the educational sphere, in the economic sphere and in the moral and religious spheres. In fact, the spirit of Gandhiji has swept over the stagnant pools of Indian national life like a tidal wave or an earthquake, removing many an old landmark and bringing into existence new configurations and new forms of life. Truly has it been said of him that he was not a man, but a phenomenon.

Gandhiji appeared on the political scene of India in 1915, when Mr. Gokhale was practically on his deathbed. Gandhiji saw at once that the type of political agitation that had been associated with the name of that great statesman could hardly serve the purpose of the nation. Till then the Indian National Congress had been following the method of constitutional agitation in accordance with the political doctrines of Victorian English Liberalism. But Gandhiji felt that for winning freedom from a foreign yoke constitutional agitation was not the method. Constitutional agitation could be effective only when there was a constitution based on the consent of the people, and if the object were merely the redress of this or that minor grievance, and not the achievement of complete national independence. But here in India was a power strongly entrenched and not founded on popular will. Gandhiji therefore felt that revolution, not reform, was the method. But, for a revolution to succeed, the people as a whole had to be roused and a spirit of sacrifice had to be fostered in them. Lokamanya Tilak had seen this. He had roused the spirit of the people and appealed to their national pride by organizing the

From D. S. Sarma, The Father of the Nation: The Life and Teachings of Mahatma Gandhi (Madras, 1956), pp. 1–21. By permission of the author.

9

Sivaji celebration and the Ganesh festivals.[1] He had gone to jail and sacrificed his life and career for the national cause. The British called him the Father of Indian Unrest. Our people, however, called him the Father of Indian Nationalism. It was the mantle of Tilak that fell on Gandhiji, and not the mantle of Gokhale, though it was Gokhale whom Gandhiji used to call his political *Guru* [teacher]. It is interesting to note that, eight years before Gandhiji appeared on the scene, Tilak, speaking in Calcutta, seemed to have forestalled the whole program of non-cooperation, which later played such an important part in the Gandhian method of attack. Speaking on the 7th January 1907, Lokamanya is reported to have said:

What the new party wants you to do is to realize the fact that your future rests entirely in your own hands. If you mean to be free, you can be free. If you do not mean to be free, you will fall and be ever fallen. So many of you need not take up arms. But, if you have not the power of active resistance, have you not the power of self-denial and self-abstinence in such a way as not to assist the foreign government to rule over you? This is boycott, and this is what is meant when we say that boycott is a political weapon. We shall not give them assistance to collect revenue and keep peace. We shall not assist them in fighting beyond our frontiers or outside India with Indian blood and money. We shall not assist them in carrying on the administration of justice. We shall have our own courts, and when the time comes, we shall not pay taxes. Can you do that by your united effort? If you can, you are free from tomorrow.

It should be remembered that this remarkable speech was delivered by Tilak eight years before Gandhiji appeared on the scene and thirteen years before he actually launched his non-cooperation movement. By a curious coincidence, on the very day on which Mahatma Gandhi inaugurated his nonviolent non-cooperation, Lokamanya Tilak breathed his last. So once again in India's history power passed from the hands of Parasurama to Sri Rama.[2] Tilak stands for Parasurama, because he believed in violence, and Gandhiji stands for Sri Rama, who, though he fought Ravana,[3] was essentially a man of peace.

Gandhiji took over from Tilak this revolutionary program of non-cooperation and made certain important and far-reaching changes. The most important change was, of course, the abandonment of violence. Tilak believed in recourse to violence. And he would not have been overscrupulous about the means to be employed against the enemy. Gandhiji, on the other hand, ruled out violence once for all from his program of political action. Nonviolence with him was not a policy, but an article of faith. Nonviolence in thought, word and deed was his motto. And, as for the means to be employed against the enemy, there was at one time a controversy between him and Tilak on the subject. Tilak relied on the old Sanskrit maxim — *S'atham prati S'aathyam* which means "Roguery towards a rogue." Gandhiji differed from him and changed the maxim into *S'atham pratyapi Satyam* which means "Truth even towards a rogue." He placed Truth and nonviolence in the forefront of his political program. For the first time in history Gandhiji raised politics to the level of religion. He says in the Introduction to his *Autobiography* that his aim in this life was *Moksha* or self-realization and that his ventures in the political world were directed to that end. He worked for *swaraj* in India, but always preferred Truth to *swaraj*. He was one of the greatest votaries of Truth who ever appeared on this earth. To him Truth was God. Hence his experiments with Truth, as he called them, were

[1] Sivaji (1627?–1680), Hindu founder of the Maratha kingdom, had challenged the authority of the Muslim rulers of the Mughal Empire. Ganesh was an elephant-headed god in the Hindu pantheon. [Editor's note]

[2] Parasurama and Rama: gods in the Hindu pantheon who figure in the epic poem, the *Ramayana*. [Editor's note]
[3] Ravana: a demon in the *Ramayana* who was defeated by Rama. [Editor's note]

conducted not in secrecy but in the open. There might be differences of opinion about the result of these experiments, but no fair-minded man could say a word against the character of the scientist who conducted them. Gandhiji's life was an open book which even a child could read.

Thus the substitution of nonviolence and truth for violence and propaganda was the most significant change that Gandhiji effected in the program of revolution. Also, he added two new features which completed the change. The first was Hindu-Muslim unity. Tilak had been considered to be anti-Muslim, because he had organized the Sivaji and Ganesh festivals and roused the religious spirit and patriotism of Hindus. Whatever that may be, we may say that Tilak was too firmly anchored in Hindu traditions and sentiments and too well aware of the history of the Mahrattas to go to the lengths to which Gandhiji was prepared to go in solving the difficult problem of Hindu-Muslim unity. He knew very well that the problem was largely the creation of the foreign bureaucracy, whose policy was to divide and rule, and that it would be difficult to induce Muslims to make common cause with Hindus. Gandhiji thought at first that the problem was easy and said that there could be no *swaraj* without Hindu-Muslim unity. And he went out of his way to respect the sentiments and safeguard the interests of Muslims. It was only towards the end of his career that he realized that the problem would remain insoluble as long as there was a third party in power in the country.

The second addition that Gandhiji made was his comprehensive, constructive program of social and economic unity. On the social side Tilak had been very conservative, and rightly so, for in his days there was a good deal of spurious social reform which only consisted in aping Western ways of living, with scant regard for the religious traditions of Hindus. Gandhiji, on the contrary, was fitted to carry out far-reaching reforms in Hindu society, for he was essentially a man of religion

and an enemy of Western civilization. His constructive program had a social side, an economic side and an educational side. On the social side he laid tremendous stress on the removal of untouchability and the elevation of the status of women. On the economic side he pleaded for the eradication of poverty in villages through the introduction of hand-spinning and weaving and the revival of village crafts. And on the educational side his program provided for a new system of education which centered round a craft and which insisted on the cultivation of both the mother tongue and a national language common to all India. We may say that in all this it was the mantle of Swami Vivekananda[4] that fell upon Gandhiji. For we know that throughout his career that great patriot-monk had pleaded passionately for the removal of the poverty and ignorance of the Indian masses and for the emancipation of Indian womanhood. Gandhiji took over, as it were, from Swami Vivekananda, his social program and added to it three original items of his own, namely, basic education, total prohibition and the cult of the spinning wheel.

Lastly, in the religious sphere we may say that it was the mantle of Sri Ramakrishna Paramahamsa [1834–1886] that fell on Gandhiji. He may not have had the spiritual realizations of the great mystic of Dakshineswar, but he taught, even as Ramakrishna did, that all religions are one, and that they are like leaves on the same tree. Sri Ramakrishna had adopted for brief periods the *sadhanas* [ways to salvation] of various religions and found by his own experience that all religions were true. Similarly, Mahatma Gandhi took his stand on the Bhagavad Gita, the Light of Asia, the New Testament, and the Koran. He associated himself with the followers of all religions on a footing of equality. At the same time, just as Sri Ramakrishna, while recog-

[4] Swami Vivekananda (1862–1902), a Hindu reformer who founded the Ramakrishna Mission to carry on social welfare work in India. [Editor's note]

nizing the unity of all religions, remained loyal to his own, so also Mahatma Gandhi, while recognizing the sanctity of all faiths, always claimed himself to be a Sanatanist [i.e., a traditional] Hindu. Sri Ramakrishna was a great devotional mystic, while Gandhiji was a great practical mystic. Our country has not produced a greater *Karma-yogin*[5] than Gandhiji. His life is the greatest commentary on the Bhagavad Gita, and unlike the learned commentaries of Sankara, Ramanuja, and Madhwa, it is a living commentary written not in words but in deeds.

Thus there is no aspect of our national life which Gandhiji has not tried to influence. Even the diet of the nation claimed his attention. He wrote many articles on diet reform advocating a balanced diet. And in his *ashramas* he incessantly carried on experiments in diet. Similarly, he was greatly interested in social hygiene, village sanitation, preservation of cattle wealth, preparation of manures and the proper disposal of night soil. In his later life he became a propagandist of Nature Cure. In fact, his speeches and writings in India from 1915 to 1947 may be said to form a veritable encyclopaedia of nation-building activities.

But it is not so much by his teachings or even by his programs that Mahatma Gandhi has influenced the masses of India as by his character. His character and personality have impressed themselves indelibly on our people's minds. They know that he is not simply a political leader or a social reformer or a friend of the poor, but first and foremost, a man of God, a saint, and *sanyasin* [religious ascetic] after their own heart. He is the embodiment of all that a Hindu admires but cannot ordinarily realize. Renunciation, self-control and penance have been the cherished ideals of Hindus from time immemorial, and here was a man who was an embodiment of these ancient virtues and who combined with them the most far-sighted statesman-

ship, the widest toleration and the tenderest love. No wonder, therefore, that the Hindus of the present day look upon him as the true descendant of their ancient *rishis* and lawgivers, reinterpreting their ancient *dharma* according to the needs of the present day and giving them a new code of conduct.

In Gandhiji we have a rare combination of the saintly and heroic types of character. He had absolute trust in God like all the great saints of the world. God always was present to his mind. He called Him his inner voice. Foreign critics may laugh at Gandhiji's inner voice, but every student of his writings knows that his inner voice was not a mere metaphor, but something very real to him. Many of his fasts, for instance, were undertaken at the bidding of that inner voice. And in most cases he never knew, even a moment before the call came, that he was going to fast. Again, not only had he absolute trust in God, but also immeasurable love towards men without any distinction of class or creed. He loved to identify himself with the lowest in the land and considered no manual labour which was the lot of any human being as something beneath himself. At one time or another in his life he actually did the work of a sweeper, a shoemaker and a scavenger. He loved to live, like the poorest peasant in India, in a hut with mud walls and floor and a thatched roof in a remote village. It is well known that during the latter part of his life he went about clad only in a loin cloth to symbolize his identification with the Indian poor. When he went to the Round Table Conference in England, he preferred to live in the East End of London amidst the poor, and in Delhi he preferred to reside in the *bhangi* (scavenger) colony.

At the same time he had no hatred or ill-will towards the rich. He was as much at home in Birla House[6] as in the *Harijan* Colony.

It is really wonderful how, in spite of

One who practices the *yoga* or discipline of action. [Editor's note]

[6] The palatial residence of G. D. Birla, a wealthy Indian industrialist. [Editor's note]

the various battles he fought in his life, he never created for himself any enemies. He tried to undermine the British Empire, but Englishmen were still his friends. He tried to undermine the authority of the South African Government, but General Smuts was nevertheless his admirer. He fought Hindu orthodoxy by his program of the removal of untouchability, and yet even orthodox Hindus called him a *Mahatma*. He undermined the position of the Indian Princes by saying that the people were the real rulers, and yet almost all the Indian Princes were his friends. This was due to the fact that everybody knew that what Gandhiji condemned was a system and not the men who happened to be associated with it. Like all saints he hated the sin and not the sinner.

Another saintly feature we discern in him is the absence of any trace of egotism. He was very much embarrassed when he was called a saint. He gave strict instructions to the inmates of his *ashram* that he should be referred to only as Gandhiji and not as Mahatma Gandhi. When he heard the report that in some place a temple had been built and his idol installed, he grew very angry and said it was an insult to him and asked the organizers to remove the idol and use the building as a spinning center. And we all know that, though he was the architect of India's freedom, he refused to take part in the celebration of the Independence Day in Delhi on the 15th August 1947, choosing to remain in Calcutta and working for communal peace there. He never claimed to be anything more than an erring mortal like all of us. He confessed his mistakes whenever he thought he had made any. Once he went so far as to say he had made a Himalayan miscalculation. And it must be admitted he miscalculated more than once the forces of evil arrayed against him.

Gandhiji was not only a saint but also a heroic fighter. It is very rarely that we find in one man a combination of the saintly and the heroic types of character. Not once or twice, but several times in his life, did Gandhiji pit his single soul against mighty odds. He pitted his soul against the South African government. He pitted his soul against the mighty British Empire. He pitted his soul against the citadel of Hindu orthodoxy. He pitted his soul against Muslim fanaticism when he travelled on foot from place to place in Noakhali.[7] Nay, he pitted his soul against Nature itself in all his celebrated fasts. All these are heroic adventures. None but a hero could stand against the organized might of an empire and against the religious fanaticism of many millions of people and go single-handed and walk straight into a lion's den of murderers and hardened ruffians.

Gandhiji combined with his heroic qualities — such as courage, determination, patience and endurance — the qualities of a great general and commander. He often led vast hordes of men along the path of danger with remarkable discipline and unity. His *satyagraha* army in South Africa, his famous Dandi March[8] and the All-India *hartals* he organized during 1919 and 1920 were something unprecedented in history. In all these cases he was able to infuse enthusiasm into thousands of men and to create heroes out of common clay and make them act with a remarkable singleness of purpose and spirit of sacrifice. His example was always catching. Many popular leaders give advice, but seldom set an example. But Gandhiji, as a rule, never asked any man to do anything which he had not done. Nor would he ever flatter the mob, as some leaders do. On the contrary, most of his speeches to the people were severe reprimands for their want of discipline, their thoughtless acts of inhumanity or selfishness as well as for their deliberate acts of wrong-doing. It was a remarkable feature of Gandhiji's leadership that he was

[7] During the period of Hindu-Muslim violence which accompanied the partition of India. [Editor's note]

[8] The "salt march" to the sea in 1930, when Gandhi launched the civil disobedience movement by breaking the law prohibiting the unlicensed manufacture of salt. [Editor's note]

able to lead and direct great mass movements without lowering any of his moral standards even by a hair's breadth. He often said he would rather be in a minority of one, so that he might follow his principles unflinchingly. He often declared that his huge following was only a hindrance to his purposes, a great burden to him and not at all a help.

*   *   *

So far we have spoken about Gandhiji as the Father of our Nation, as the architect of India's freedom, as a great saint, a great hero, a great general and a kindly patriarch. But he is greater still. He is not only all these but also an apostle of peace and nonviolence. He is a man with a divine mission. He has an exalted place not only in the History of Mankind. This is his highest glory. Here it is the mantle of Buddha, the world-renowned Prince of Peace, that has fallen on the shoulders of Mahatma Gandhi. In India, in spite of all our defeats and humiliations, in spite of the defects of our national character and the drawbacks of our civilization, there has been a steady progress in nonviolence from the Vedas to the Upanishads, from the Upanishads to the Gita, from the Gita to Buddha and from Buddha to Gandhi. . . .

Coming in the footsteps of the Gita and Buddha, Gandhiji says in our day:

I am not a visionary. I claim to be a practical idealist. The religion of nonviolence is not merely for the *rishis* and saints. It is meant for the common people as well. Nonviolence is the law of our species, as violence is the law of the brute.

. . . Gandhi, the greatest apostle of nonviolence and peace in modern times, ranks among the saviours of mankind. For mankind seems to have come to a great crisis in its history. Unless it accepts the gospel of nonviolence as preached by Gandhiji and gives up war and violence as a means of settlement of disputes great or small, there seems to be little hope for it in the conditions under which modern wars are being waged. . . . Unless all the evolution on this planet is going to end in a fiasco, mankind must accept the gospel of nonviolence. . . . Future generations will remember [Gandhi] not so much as the architect of India's freedom, not so much as a saint or hero, but as one of the saviours of mankind, in the same rank as Buddha and Christ.

One may ask, "Has Mahatma Gandhi succeeded in gaining his objectives in this generation?" The answer to this question is both "Yes" and "No." He has succeeded in winning *swaraj* for India. He has succeeded in rousing the social conscience of Hindus and discrediting the age-long evil practice of Untouchability. He has succeeded in revitalizing the faith of his countrymen in their own ancient culture and its spiritual values. He has succeeded in setting before the nation a model of the perfect *Karma-yogin* described in the *Bhagavad Gita*. But these were only his lower objectives. His higher and main objective was to make his countrymen accept nonviolence as the law of life in all their activities and to lay the foundations in India of a nonviolent state of village republics possessing no military force and no large-scale industrial machinery. In this he may be said to have failed completely, as his countrymen did not rise to the occasion and carry out his teaching. Far from fulfilling his expectations, we may say they sank even lower than before, when we take into account the appalling outrages and bloodshed which preceded and followed the partition of India. For a time violence stalked the land naked and unashamed, and at last carried off the great Apostle of Nonviolence himself. This showed how grievously the *Mahatma* had miscalculated the forces of evil arrayed against him and how greatly he had exaggerated to himself the capacities of his countrymen. The fact is that Mahatma Gandhi was centuries ahead of common humanity in his moral evolution and was bound to fail in carrying them along with him. But he has sown the good seed and it is our faith that it will sprout and grow and yield fruit in God's good time. Meanwhile it is the sacred duty of India to strengthen herself in every way and guard the priceless gift of freedom be- queathed to her by the Fath[ ] tion and gradually march tow[ ] he has set before her.

The Revolutionary Significance of Gandhi

HUMAYUN KABIR

Humayun Kabir (1906–   ) is a distinguished Indian writer and political figure whose background lies in the Muslim tradition rather than that of Hinduism. He has held posts in the government of India as Minister of Civil Aviation (1957–58) and Minister for Scientific Research and Cultural Affairs (1958–   ), and is the author of more than a dozen volumes in such diverse fields as poetry, philosophy, history, and education. His appreciation of Gandhi in the article which follows reveals the mark which Gandhi made on Indians of all classes and creeds.

PERHAPS never before in history did an inhabitant of a dependent country achieve such position and prestige in the contemporary world as Mohandas Karamchand Gandhi. He was honoured not only as a great statesman and political leader but as a leader of thought with a new message for mankind. The principles of Christianity provide the basis of modern European civilization. Yet Westerners themselves admit that these principles were more faithfully followed by this half-naked Fakir of the East than by any individual of the Western world.

East and West, however, unite in recognizing in Gandhiji one of the strongest characters of the modern age. Even those who sought to defy or repudiate him could [not] deny the power of his personality. What then was the secret of his strength? There are among his admirers some who think that his power and influence were derived from spiritual and super-normal sources which defy analysis. This, however, is hardly any answer. For whatever its ori-

gin, his power operated on the plane of material facts and natural events. Nor is this surprising, for even superhuman power requires for its manifestation a human background and field of activity. The strength of Gandhiji must, therefore, be understood in human terms.

Gandhiji's revolutionary significance lay in his attempt to release the energies contained in the endurance of the Indian people. This he sought to do by his complete identification with the average Indian. It was from his strong sense of unity with the starving, naked and ignorant masses of India that he derived his own power. And by his identification with them he sought to transfer some of that power to the masses themselves. The contrast between the energy he displayed and their passivity is at first baffling, but this contrast itself gives a clue to the understanding of his power and his influence.

He was, however, not content to change the texture of the Indian mind alone; he felt he had a message for the entire world.

From Humayun Kabir, "Gandhiji and the Indian Revolution," in *Gandhi Memorial Peace Number, The Visva-Bharati Quarterly*, Kshitis Roy, ed. (Santiniketan, India, 1949), pp. 212–229. By permission of the author.

.nough he may not have succeeded in transforming the universe, he has everywhere stirred the mind of man. Complete success in such endeavors is perhaps, from the nature of the case, unattainable. The achievement of Indian freedom and its repercussions throughout the world prove that his endeavors have not been without avail.

Before launching the struggle for liberation, Gandhiji had to forge a weapon of proved temper. This was a difficult task on account of the loss of spiritual unity from which the Indian people suffered. The impact of the West had sundered their unity so that Indians found themselves a people of divided consciousness. The classes and the masses had drifted from one another till they had hardly any point of contact. Gandhiji set [out] to restore the points of contact and reestablish unity. This marked his greatest political effort and made him a revolutionary leader of the first importance.

Gandhiji was born at a time when the magnificence of British power had dazzled the Indian intellect. It influenced even the feelings and the will of the people. The memories of the struggle of 1857 had not yet faded out of public consciousness. Its effects were however dissipated as different communities reacted differently to it. The Indian Muslims were divided, inactive, and full of bitterness. Among the Hindus, feelings were divided. Some felt bitter, but for others there was no sense of defeat or frustration. Smaller communities like the Parsis or the Sikhs felt they had a share in the British victory of 1857. The political leadership of the British was accepted almost as an axiom not only in India but outside. It was the heyday of British glory and *pax britannica* ruled the world.

The modern era of scientific advance had begun. It opened to man a new world of immense possibilities. On the material plane, it led to an unprecedented development in technology. On the intellectual plane, it gave rise to nineteeth century rationalism. On the political plane, its finest manifestation was liberal democracy in the Nation State. There seemed no barrier to human progress, and it seemed that with spread of education, all human ills would be resolved. It was an era of expansion, buoyancy and faith in reason.

The prospect of endless progress inspired Indian intellectuals as well. They derived their inspiration from Britain and shared the British faith in science and democracy. European influence transcended the intellectual plane and affected the world of their emotions. Even Indian aspirations for freer and fuller life acquired a European tone. British cooperation and help were regarded as necessary elements in any endeavor for liberty.

The Indian intellectuals were so dazzled by European civilization that they attempted to transplant wholesale the culture of Europe to Indian soil. They hardly thought in terms of synthesis, for synthesis implies mutual give and take. To the Anglophile, there was little that India could give. For them, India's function was only to receive. The vast masses of Indians did not, however, feel that way. They had an instinctive sense of the value of their culture and resisted attempts at disrupting it. The Anglophile, therefore, sought to create an Indo-Anglian culture without the cooperation of the Indian people themselves. Such attempts at achieving a new culture had no roots in the life of the people. It was therefore not at all surprising that the forms and conventions of Indo-Anglian society soon became objects of ridicule.

That he diverted the energy and direction of Indian politics from Europe to India was Gandhiji's greatest achievement. Instead of attempting an Ersatz Europe, he sought to build up a genuine India. There were distinguished Indians who had worked for the people even before he appeared on the scene. They, however, served from a pedestal of superiority and stooped only to conquer. This feeling of superiority prevented them from identifying themselves with the masses. In consequence, before the advent of Gandhiji, political activities and movements in India centered mainly round the middle and upper classes. The dumb, inert and inactive Indian people hardly understood them and did little to respond to their appeal. At best, they were silent spectators: at worst, sullen opponents of what they regarded as interference with the beneficent activities of the administration.

The restoration of spiritual community between the classes and the masses was Gandhiji's first objective, but it was not an easy task. The first step towards its achievement had to be the realization of a common life. Gandhiji's first demand on Indian political workers proved the genius of the man. He declared that they must in mode of conduct and life, speech and thought, habit and clothing, food and habitation identify themselves with the starving, naked and illiterate masses of Indian humanity. He adopted the language of the people for all political transactions. His mode of life was hardly distinguishable from that of the Indian peasant.

The response of the masses was unprecedented and almost unbelievable. They hailed Gandhiji as their own leader and representative — a leader who spoke their language, wore their clothes, ate their food. The alien imperialist sought to ridicule him as a half-naked Fakir.[1] Such ridicule was only evidence of the obtuseness and stupidity of those who indulged in it. The scoffer did not realize that what he regarded as a cause for ridicule was in fact the secret of Gandhiji's hold over the Indian people.

This, however, is not the only evidence of Gandhiji's genius. He sought to transform India's weakness itself into a source of strength by transmuting the inertia and inaction of the Indian character. Before his advent, the constitution of the Indian masses was such that there was hardly any possibility of an active and energetic revolution in India. Gandhiji did not quarrel with facts. He sought to use them for his own purposes. He accepted the fatalism and passivity of the Indian people but found for them a new political function. Instead of an aggressive and militant struggle, he built up a movement of non-cooperation in which passivity and endurance were turned into sources of strength and energy.

The attempt to re-integrate the social and political outlook of India was only one phase of the Gandhian experiment with truth. His more fundamental urge was to evolve a new conception of Society and the State. He sought to reconcile the traditions of the Indian people with the requirements of the modern age, and find in this reconciliation a solution of the ills of the modern world. His claim to leadership in thought is based on this outline of a new philosophy of life and action. Traditional modes of Western thought had led to a dead end, but his experiments seemed to suggest a way out of the prevailing political and social impasse.

The cause of Europe's malaise was her inability to profit by her own experience. The eighteenth and the nineteenth centuries taught men that political freedom often conceals economic slavery of the worst type. Political democracy permitted the employment of children under twelve in hard labor for sixteen continuous hours. Not only permitted, but defended such exploitation on the plea of freedom of contract and the right of the individual to sell his labor as he liked. Lawyers, politicians, doctors and even bishops came forward to justify it on legal, political, medical and religious grounds. Such iniquity could not continue indefinitely, and early in the nineteenth century the demand

---

[1] The reference is to Winston Churchill's comment, at the time of the Gandhi-Irwin talks in 1931, on "the nauseating and humiliating spectacle of this one-time Inner Temple lawyer, now seditious fakir, striding half-naked up the steps of the Viceroy's palace, there to negotiate and to parley on equal terms with the representative of the King-Emperor." [Editor's note]

arose for a limitation on the freedom of contract. That the state must assure the individual not only the forms of political liberty but the content of economic freedom became the new battle-cry.

The contention that only a state and a society which guarantee freedom from want and fear can claim the allegiance of man was accepted by everyone in theory. The unanimity disappeared when men thought in terms of ways and means to realize that end. The liberal rationalist saw the possibility of progress in the improvement of existing modes of production and the general extension of education and the franchise. The socialist repudiated the individual's right to profit at the cost of the community and sought the millennium by a gradual transformation of prevalent social forms through the extension of the power of the state. The revolutionary anarchist found the promise of a new heaven in his ideal of abolition of the state.

All these modes of thought left their mark on Gandhiji's mental make-up. Their conflict and discrepancy provoked him to attempt his own synthesis. His philosophy of life evolved as a result of his attempt to reconcile these conflicting claims against the background of Indian history and tradition. This integration of Western cross-currents into an Indian background explains the revolutionary possibilities in Gandhiji's social and political thought.

The experience of the modern world proves that total rejection of industrial and machine civilization is altogether impossible. The application of science to the satisfaction of our needs is helping us to overcome climatic and physical disabilities. Applied Sciences may at first serve only a few in society but invariably its application is extended. Ultimately it can and often does benefit every single individual of the world. Machine is therefore a common servant. Only its misuse can lead to private benefit at the cost of the community. Use of machine leads to increase of common wealth and its abuse to concentration of wealth in single hands. This, however,

is not the fault of the machine but of the men who abuse it and degrade men. Gandhiji's repugnance to the machine was not a repudiation of the machine as such but only a protest against such debasement of humanity.

A little reflection makes this clear. The spinning wheel and the oil press are also machines. No doubt, they are small and worked through human or animal power, but this does not change their character as machinery. There is, however, reason for Gandhiji's suspicions of large-scale machinery. When the machine is worked by human power, it is directly under human control. Even the possibility of its abuse is strictly limited. With large-scale machinery it is different. Man himself tends to become a cog in the machine. In any case, it develops an impersonal character in which the human may easily be overlooked. The process tends to become more important than the produce or even the producer. Slowly the machine dehumanizes man.

It was this danger inherent in large-scale industrialization that led Gandhiji to conceive of the autonomous and self-contained village as the unit of society. As far as possible, every village must regulate its own economic and political life. In such small units, the human relationship between individuals would be strong. It could never be replaced by merely mechanical and impersonal relationships. In village communities, there would be scope for individual freedom. There would, however, be no risk of its degeneration into license or anarchy. The absolute dictatorship of the state and the absolute anarchy of statelessness are both attended with many risks. In the small village community, men could avoid both these dangers and carry liberal democracy to its logical conclusion.

A new type of civilization must avoid the defects inherent in rural economy and the pitfalls revealed in the working of modern civilization. The petty jealousies and wastefulness of village life as well as the soulless aridity and formlessness of urban society must be overcome if the individual is to achieve the full measure of his personality. The village is personal and intimate to the point of interference with one's private life. The city is impersonal and indifferent to the point of callousness. The defects of both must be avoided if the future civilization of the world is to permit the free growth of the individual in free society. The evolution of a new culture in which the best elements of the past and the present will be fused demands keenness of the mind, catholicity of heart and resilience of spirit.

In the past, expansion in the scale of production inevitably provoked an expansion in the size of cities. Man's limited power required aggregation in large numbers to make an increase in the standard of life possible. Higher standards depended upon more commodities and more commodities upon larger units of production. Today, with the substitution of electricity for steam as the main source of energy, all this has changed. Where electricity is the motive power, the concentration of multitudes in industrial town and slums is no longer inevitable. Electricity makes the distribution of industry over a large area possible. It offers a possibility of restoring conditions analogous to those which obtained in the days of rural crafts. It promises to combine the finest elements in the rural and the civic cultures of the past. Rich human relations can now be combined with increase in the riches of the world. Deep emotional vitality side by side with conditions of plenty for everybody can release human energies for new creative ventures. A dim awareness of this possibility was a factor behind Gandhiji's insistence upon decentralization of industry and the creation of small and autonomous units.

Experience of European civilization made Gandhiji realize the importance of the economic independence of the individual. Without it, political independence often becomes a mockery and democracy a mere form. He also saw that undue concentration of wealth undermined the economic independence of the individual, and yet followed almost inevitably from large-scale production under private proprietary right. His analysis so far was identical with that of Socialism. His solution was, however, different from theirs. The socialist remedy was and is to eliminate private property while Gandhiji found the solution in dispersal of industry.

The difference in the socialist and the Gandhian solution is not difficult to understand. Socialists are prepared to impose equality — political and economic and social — by violence if necessary. Gandhiji, however, felt that equality which is the basis of economic independence must be achieved through peaceful and nonviolent methods. Political liberty may be and has often been achieved through bloody revolution. This, however, has, in Gandhiji's opinion, brought the form and not the substance of freedom. Those who have taken to the sword have more often than not perished by the sword. Besides, the results of violent revolution are always liable to be lost by a violent counterrevolution. It was because of his awareness of this danger that Gandhiji urged that the economic and political freedom of man must be attained through a conquest of hatred. What is achieved by persuasion is less likely to be upset by force.

Gandhiji appeared in an India where political activity was restricted to petitions and prayers to the British authorities. He changed all this, for he discovered in Indian traditions a technique of struggle suited to the land. He did not overlook the disabilities under which he had to work, but neither did he allow them to overawe and immobilize him. He knew that regeneration must be a slow process, for a people weakened and emasculated through the oppression of centuries could not be inured to sacrifice and hardship overnight. Gandhiji's first task was to revive the spirit of self-respect of the Indian people. Once this was done, resistance to evil would be easy. The first task he set his followers was the comparatively easy one of over-

coming the fear of arrest and imprisonment. Comparatively easier, no doubt, but
an extremely difficult thing in the prevailing temper of the day. Imprisonment
was a stigma and man avoided it more than
crime. Gandhiji transformed Indian politics by his deliberate defiance of unaccept-
able laws with a full consciousness of the
possible consequences. It is now difficult
to remember the fear and nervousness
which jail life then had for the average
citizen. Imprisonment for a political cause
carries with it an element of martyrdom in
contemporary India. By overcoming the
fear of jail, Gandhiji wrought a psychological revolution whose extent we can
hardly realize today.

Once the fear of jail had disappeared,
Gandhiji felt the time had come for a second step. His aim this time was to free the
people from the fear of loss of property.
After their experience of the non-cooperation movement [the British] discovered
that it was more effective to hit the pocket
than the person. People who thought little
of imprisonment or even physical assault
hesitated when it meant permanent impoverishment. The civil disobedience movement of 1930 sought to destroy this fear of
impoverishment and loss of property. Large
numbers of men and women responded
to his call, and for a time it seemed as if
the national struggle had attained its goal.
Gandhiji knew better and was not yet prepared to overstrain his sense of realism. . . .

The third and final step in this process
of strengthening the nation's fiber was the
most difficult. The fear of jail had been
overcome. Large numbers had learnt to
conquer the lure of property. A generation
had grown up who refused to be daunted
by the threat of poverty. To risk one's life
is, however, another matter. Gandhiji knew
that this supreme test must be imposed
only when the conditions promised victory. These conditions were created after
the outbreak of the war in 1939. The war
not only created an appropriate situation
but also compelled a struggle for the nation's emancipation. Liberty was in danger

all over the world and India was called
upon to succour it. How could a nation
fight for the maintenance of others' freedom when it was itself in bondage? Shat-
tering of India's bonds became necessary
not only in her own interest but for the
sake of the freedom of the world. It was
then and then alone that Gandhiji gave
the call of "Do or Die."

There are devotees of Marx who profess that Gandhiji betrayed the struggle
for Indian independence, not once, not
twice, but on three different occasions —
in 1922, in 1931 and again in 1939 on the
outbreak of the war. They characterize the
suspension of the non-cooperation movement after the Chauri Chaura incident [2]
as deliberate sabotage. They say,

Gandhiji did not want the movement to attain
complete success. He knew that this could be
done only through revolutionary methods.
Once, however, the people resorted to revolutionary action, they would sweep away not
only British Imperialism but also the vested
interests of the propertied classes. This Gandhiji did not want. That is why his political
moves were aimed at putting pressure on the
British but not at liquidating the existing regime. That is also why he suspended the non-
cooperation movement when it was on the
verge of success, for he feared that once the
masses had tasted victory, they would not stop
with political change but [would] go on to
transform the economic structure of society.

These pseudo-Marxists are not alone in
condemning Gandhiji for suspending the
non-cooperation movement. There are
others also who hold that it was not the
initiation but the suspension of the non-
cooperation that was a Himalayan blunder.
They argue that in such a vast uprising of
an entire people, incidents like Chauri
Chaura cannot be altogether ruled out.
They further say that violence and nonviolence are relative terms, and should be

[2] In 1922 the plan to launch mass civil disobedience in the Bardoli subdivision of Bombay Presidency was abruptly suspended after an outbreak
of violence in the village of Chauri Chaura in the
United Provinces. [Editor's note]

judged not on theoretical grounds but considerations of practical expediency.

Whatever be the objective justification for such criticism, the critics show an utter failure to understand Gandhiji's mind. For him, nonviolence is a supreme value and is the standard by which our action must be judged. He did not recognize the distinction of means and ends. For him considerations of practical expediency were, therefore, utterly irrelevant. He valued the individual in and for himself and believed that the freedom of the individual could be attained only through the discipline of nonviolence. In mob frenzy the individual surrenders his independence. The incursion of mob frenzy into political action meant for Gandhiji the end of the struggle for freedom. Whether we accept his contention or not, we must admit that in suspending the non-cooperation movement, he acted consistently with his own principles. After Chauri Chaura, Gandhiji, on his own premises, had no other alternative.

Those who claim to be students of Marx, are in any case not entitled to criticise Gandhiji. They proclaim their belief in historical necessity and hold that unalterable economic laws guide the destinies of man. How then can they consistently say that Gandhiji prevented the achievement of Indian independence in 1922 by his decision to suspend the non-cooperation movement? They are not prepared to give Gandhiji credit for the awakening of the masses. They say that it was inevitable in the circumstances of the day, and dismiss Pandit Nehru's devotion to Gandhiji as superstitious hero-worship. If it is superstitious to believe that an individual can bring about the freedom of a country, is it not equally superstitious to hold that a single individual can prevent the realization of its freedom?

The true explanation of Gandhiji's decision after Chauri Chaura can be found in the course of events itself. An inert people had been moved, but the inertia of ages could not be fully dissolved so soon. Even a machine has to be carefully handled while it is new and gradually geared into use. With so delicate an organism as a newly awakened nation, the early stage required even more careful and gentle handling. With his intimate knowledge and deep community of spirit with the masses, Gandhiji realized that it would be a mistake to put too severe a strain on their newly found strength. It was enough that the masses had shaken off their fear of jail. In spite of spasmodic outbursts of mass frenzy, they were not yet ready to sacrifice life or even property for the achievement of their goal. The first lesson in struggle and sacrifice must necessarily stop short of the supreme test.

The same considerations weighed with Gandhiji at the time of the pact with Irwin.[3] It is true that the nation had responded magnificently to his call. Vast numbers of common men and women had overcome not only the fear of jail but also the attachment to wealth and property. They made sacrifices with a sense of exultation and clamored to make still greater sacrifices. To a superficial observer it might well have seemed that India's hour of destiny had struck.

Gandhiji, however, knew better. He knew that though large numbers had responded to his call, still larger numbers were yet inert and passive. Besides, the enthusiasm that had been evoked was sporadic and transient. The devotion which works steadily from year to year and slowly wears out the stiffest of obstacles was not yet in evidence. He felt that it was wiser to compromise while yet there was a chance of victory. The disposition of forces on both sides favoured the British if the struggle was prolonged. There was of course the possibility that if it could be prolonged long enough, the advantage would again shift over in favour of the Indian people. Gandhiji was not sure if the newly

[3] In 1931, at the height of the civil disobedience movement, Gandhi met with the viceroy, Lord Irwin, and agreed to suspend civil disobedience and to attend the next session of the Round Table Conference in London. [Editor's note]

awakened masses were sufficiently strengthened in gristle to continue the struggle long enough. He decided to call a truce and the Gandhi-Irwin pact marked the height of Congress achievement in the days before the attainment of freedom.

The utter unreality of this so-called Marxist criticism is however seen most clearly in their attack on Gandhiji for not having launched what the critics would call a revolutionary mass struggle at the outset of the recent war. They contend that the British, embroiled in a life and death struggle, could not have resisted India's challenge in 1939. In their anxiety to exaggerate England's difficulties, they, however, overlook some of the most important aspects of the situation. England, no doubt, faced a mortal threat but she still had intact her vast resources scattered throughout the world. On the other hand, conditions in India hardly favored a fight. For Gandhiji the moral issues were supreme, but even if he had ignored them, expediency dictated the same course of action as morality. In his long experience of the Indian masses, Gandhiji had found that a political struggle gathered strength only when it was based upon economic distress. The outbreak of the war brought in the country economic prosperity, though this was, from the nature of the case, bound to be short-lived.

A struggle in 1939 would have taken place against a background of rising prices and wages. Prices of raw materials were sharply rising. The peasant was on the whole satisfied because of the increase in the price of agricultural goods. Labor was also for the moment satisfied, as the increase in wages more than compensated at this stage the rise in the cost of living. In the peculiar context of India, an alien government took good care to see that these two classes did not have any special cause for grievance. Economic scarcity would no doubt grow, as more and more of the nation's energies was diverted to war purposes. For the time being, however, these two classes were able to achieve a slight increase in their standard of life.

A general must base his strategy on facts as they exist. The prosperity of the peasant and the working classes might be spurious and short-lived, but so long as it was there, it was doubtful if they would respond to the call for struggle. There was in addition a new source of weakness on account of the growing communal regimentation of the people. The working of provincial autonomy without the framework of an all-India Federation had released fissiparous forces and encouraged the growth of communal and provincial fragmentation. There was even a risk that the launching of a struggle might serve as the signal for the outbreak of communal strife. It was almost certain that in the context of a war situation, the British would not hesitate to use any element that promised some diversion in the national struggle.

Nor could Gandhiji forget that any struggle launched in 1939 would take place under conditions of war. The previous struggles for freedom had all taken place during periods of peace and had to face the rigors imposed by a civil administration. During war, the government would not hesitate to resort to military administration and martial law. The risks implicit in the struggle would therefore be far greater and could be justified only if the Indian masses were economically and politically hardened enough to fight on more than one front.

Gandhiji knew that against the background of the war, the struggle would be bitter and might be long. In any case, it would not permit any heroics. He, therefore, wanted to test the quality of the nation before taking the irrevocable step. The experiment with selected individuals in 1940 was thus only a preparation for a larger struggle.

The crisis of the war was reached in 1942. In the international field, the contending parties held one another in a precarious balance. Both the contestants had deployed their full strength and were susceptible to the slightest alteration in the disposition of their forces. Within India, rising prices had at last left rising wages far behind. Growing scarcity of consumable goods compelled a diminution in the general standard of life. The increasing economic and political difficulties had turned the mind of the people from their communal and provincial wrangles to the supreme necessity of achieving freedom, here and now. Internally and externally, the stage was set for India's fight for liberty and once more it was Gandhiji who gave the call.

The rising of 1942 was a revolution without a plan. The British dared not allow Gandhiji time to develop his strategy. Experience had taught them that he was superb in opening a campaign. Unless apprehended before his movement had gathered momentum, he might prove well nigh unconquerable. Twice they had learnt that while he was at it, they could not afford to laugh even at seeming trivialities. Against the background of the war, they could not afford to take chances. They clapped into prison the entire leadership of the Congress even before the movement was launched.

What shape or course the Revolution of 1942 would have taken if Gandhiji had remained at the helm must remain a matter for conjecture. One thing alone is certain. He was wedded to nonviolence and was not prepared to compromise on a principle for any immediate gain. At the same time, he regarded the struggle of 1942 as the final stage in the fight for India's freedom. Even his slogan was different this time. "Do or Die," he said, but even the urgency of this last struggle could not make him say, "Kill or die."

To all outward appearances, the struggle of 1942 failed. Within three months, the mass uprising was crushed and law and order reimposed upon the land. Corruption was rampant. Famine stalked the land. The war effort continued. Gandhiji and his colleagues ate out their heart behind the prison bars. And the people were denied even the knowledge of their whereabouts.

The triumph of imperialism was, however, more apparent than real. "Quit India" said Gandhiji and a million voices took up the cry. "Do or die" said the Leader and thousands literally laid down their lives in their effort to achieve freedom. The earlier movements had taught the people to overcome the fear of jail and the fear of poverty. This last and greatest movement of all taught his followers to shed fear of death.

When the individual is prepared to lay down his life, the community cannot die. Gandhiji taught the common man in India to overcome the fear of death. The British realized the significance of the lesson before the average Indian. Supreme realists as they are, they knew that the days of their empire were over. They decided to go while the going was still good. Gandhiji had achieved something that had never before been attempted in history: the liberation of a people without resort to armed insurrection and violent strife.

With the achievement of freedom, Gandhiji's life-work in the field of politics was accomplished. Not, however, in the field of social and moral uplift of the people. In these fields he rose to his supremest height after 15th August 1947. The joy in the attainment of freedom was marred by the division of the country. Partition brought in its train conflict and carnage. Freedom had been bought at the cost of unity and peace.

The light of humanity grew dim over vast areas in the Indian subcontinent. On both sides of the newly created and artificial borders, hatred and fury blinded men. And even more than hatred and fury, fear. Man was afraid of man as never before in Indian history. The masses were swayed by a mad frenzy which threatened to destroy the bastions of society. The artificial political division led to a fragmentation of human personality itself. The same man was often steeped in shameful deeds of darkness and lifted to unbelievable heights of heroism and magnanimity.

When everything was uncertain and fluid, and men seemed to be threatened with the loss of humanity, Gandhiji stood like a pillar of rock. Like a beacon in the darkness, his message illumined the darkest corners of the soul. Reason and charity were his watchwords. Even from those who had suffered unspeakable sorrow and humiliation he demanded tolerance, goodwill and love. He challenged their manhood and declared that to debase human standards was worse than death. He denounced private vengeance and retaliation which violate man's inmost nature and destroy the very basis of society. So long as he lived, the forces of evil feared that they could not triumph. It was, therefore, not surprising that they should strike at him and seek to quench the light which held at bay the gathering darkness.

Evil struck at him and killed his mortal body, but his message it could not kill. Liberated from physical bonds, his spirit strode the world and achieved a power which in his life he had never enjoyed. His death vindicated his life, and in death he triumphed even as another who conquered the world by laying down his life two thousand years ago.

An Englishman's Tribute

HORACE ALEXANDER

To some Englishmen, Gandhi appeared as an enemy; there were others, however, to whom he was a man to be admired and praised. In the following selection, Horace Alexander (1889–   ), author, teacher, and member of the Society of Friends, gives a sympathetic appreciation of the man he felt privileged to call his friend.

INDIA today, . . . the India that is neither a return to the Vedas nor a pale reflection of the West, is essentially the creation of Gandhi.

Gandhi called himself a Hindu to the day of his death. He never changed his religious loyalty. When he was in South Africa, as a young man, he was intimate with evangelically-minded Christians, who for a time influenced him so much that he seriously considered "conversion". . . . But, on full consideration, the young Gandhi decided that there was no reason to cut himself away from his Hindu roots. If Christianity had something to teach Hinduism, then he, as a Hindu, must try to purify Hinduism — for example, by fighting the curse of Untouchability. . . .

Gandhi is the central figure in the new Indian culture; and one essential thing about him is that, while remaining a Hindu all his life, he welcomed and tried to make his own the best in every religious tradition. A century before Gandhi, Ram Mohan Roy, the first inspirer of Indian social reform, gave himself to the study of Persian and of the Koran in his early manhood. It might fairly be argued that Ram Mohan Roy did more to Islamize the Hinduism of Bengal in the early nineteenth

From Horace Alexander, *Consider India: An Essay in Values* (Bombay, 1961), pp. 39–42, 45, 59–61, 67–70, 73–74. By permission of Asia Publishing House.

century than to Christianize it. At any rate, as far as he could, he did both. But when we come to Gandhi a still more potent Muslim influence suggests itself. Gandhi, in the last phase of his life, began to use a word *sarvodaya* to express his social philosophy. This word, as far as I know, was coined by him to translate the idea conveyed in the title of John Ruskin's essay, "Unto this Last." At least it means the same thing: the good of all, as opposed to ideas of the greatest good of the greatest number: not the majority, says Gandhi, not even a ninety-nine per cent majority, but *all* must be the concern of the true welfare State. Where did Gandhi get this idea? He may have found it in many places —Ruskin, Rousseau, the New Testament, the Gita, and so on; but surely in part, perhaps even principally, it stems from the Islamic conception of human brotherhood, in which every man is equal in the sight of God. This conception, so alien to the Hindu caste structure, can hardly have come to India from western Christianity, though it is easy enough to find it in the Gospels. Politically, India no doubt has derived the idea of equality largely from the influence of the French and American Revolutions; but in the more fundamental human and religious sense, it has come through Gandhi, and it would seem that he derived it primarily from Islam.

Here are Gandhi's own words about Islam: "Islam's distinctive contribution to India's national culture," he wrote in *Young India* in 1929, "is its unadulterated belief in the oneness of God and a practical application of the truth of the brotherhood of man for those who are nominally within its fold. I call these two distinctive contributions. For in Hinduism the spirit of brotherhood has become too much philosophized. Similarly, though philosophical Hinduism has no other god but God, it cannot be denied that practical Hinduism is not so emphatically uncompromising as Islam. . . ."

Let it never be thought that for Gandhi religion was chiefly a matter of "religions" or of speculation on the nature of the absolute, however profound and truly philosophical. Reginald Reynolds has recently written that Gandhi "emphasized work as worship, community as religion, right action as true idealism." The religious man, in Gandhi's estimation, was not the man who either preached stirring sermons or listened to them, or who faithfully carried out so-called religious practices. Rather, he was the man who lost himself in devotion to the service of humanity.

* * *

Although this is not primarily a study of politics, Gandhi's part in the liberation of India from British rule is so important that it seems appropriate to draw attention here to the real significance of what happened. Some Britishers are inclined to argue that Gandhi, far from helping forward the process of self-government, actually retarded it. The British government, it is pointed out, had always declared that self-government was the end at which they aimed. India was being prepared for this by successive stages; first municipal self-government, then provincial self-government, and finally the transfer of power at the center was bound to follow. If only Indians would work the new representative institutions with energy and goodwill, the transfer would come speedily.

During the Round Table Conference on the future of Indian government, held in London in the autumn of 1931, Gandhi spent a weekend in the Master's Lodge, at Balliol College, Oxford, meeting informally several leading British public men, official and unofficial, in an endeavour to break the deadlock between the British government and the Indian National Congress. Professor Coupland opened the session by expounding the theory that, in the development of the British Commonwealth of free nations, freedom had broadened down from precedent to precedent in an orderly manner, stage by stage, until in turn Canada, Australia, New Zealand, South Africa and Ireland had all achieved full freedom; and that the more orderly and constitutional the movement in each domain had been, the more rapid had been the development. In a sentence, the British people responded to constitutional appeals, especially when they were backed by efficient discharge of local self-government, whereas they only had their backs put up, and were liable to take a stiff and uncompromising line of resistance, if any kind of pressure through direct action were attempted.

Gandhi listened respectfully, but he proceeded to assure Professor Coupland that he considered him wrong in both history and psychology. He pointed out that the Canadian Rebellion [of 1837] was the shock that led the British people to recognize the need for self-government in Canada. The history of both Ireland and South Africa demonstrated the same thesis. In both cases, after much talk of self-government, it only finally arrived after bloody conflict, when the British people had seen that it could no longer be denied. Even in New Zealand, there had been a Maori Rebellion. Australia alone had come to full self-government in the manner the Professor had suggested was typical. Gandhi went on to say that he did not suggest that the British people meanly surrendered to armed force. On the contrary, they might begin by suppressing the rebellion. But they learnt to respect a nation, when they saw that it was so determined to have its freedom that it was willing to fight and die in the attempt to achieve it. He was convinced that the same would prove true in the case of India. The only way India could achieve real freedom was not by having it handed to them from Britain bit by bit, but by fighting for it, and earning the respect of the British in the process. Only, they meant their fight, unlike the Canadian, Irish and South African fightings, to be nonviolent, so that the Indians would suffer most, and the English as little as possible.

* * *

[Gandhi's] immense belief in the dignity and strength of a fearless man governed his thought in the economic field no less than the political. He perceived that it is the peasant, the cultivator of the soil, who silently keeps the world alive through times of war and conquest and pestilence. From time to time a whole countryside may be devastated by the scourge of famine or disease or by the sword of a conqueror; but unless the land becomes infertile and reverts to desert, as soon as the pestilence of disease or conquest passes, men return to the land and begin to plough it and sow it and reap crops again. So is the world maintained. It was therefore the dumb millions of food-producing peasants who were Gandhi's chief concern and on whose backs he built his hopes.

In India he found a peasantry whose independence was largely undermined. The British had taught them not to think for themselves, and not to be self-dependent for their clothes and their tools. "We command, you obey," said the British, "for we know what is good for you; we will supply you with better clothes and tools than you can make, and you can buy them at world-market prices." "But you need not obey," said Gandhi, "you can be wholly independent. Moreover, if you make your own clothes and your own tools, you will be beginning the fight against your abject poverty. You can do it for yourselves." So he evolved a "constructive program," which ignored the alien ruler and laid the foundations of political independence on the firm base of economic independence. Let each village first learn to live as an independent unit, feeding itself, making its own clothes from its own cotton, providing its own housing and its own essential tools; then, when it has an upright backbone of its own, it can go on to an honest exchange of goods and services with neighbouring villages, with far away cities, even with the ends of the earth.

It should be noted here that Gandhi was not, as Western people commonly suppose, opposed to all machinery and to all industrialization. The spinning wheel itself, which he asked every Indian to ply, was, as he freely admitted, a machine. He was an enthusiast for the sewing machine, which he regarded as a true labor-saving device. . . . Gandhi's objection was to the craze for machinery — a craze comparable to the addict's constant yearning for more cigarettes or more alcohol or more opium. The test of every new invention should be: Is it really the servant of man — not just to make a few men richer while others become slaves to the machine or are thrown out of work. Far better that thousands of men should carry heavy loads on their heads up steep banks to build a great dam rather than that the work should all be done by great cranes while the men and their families sit idle and starve in their villages. And today in India those are the only alternatives. In twenty years' time the economy may have been so transformed that more labor-saving machinery will be good for India. Gandhi utterly repudiated the argument that the cheapest way of producing goods was necessarily the most economic from the point of view of general human well-being; and it is human well-being, not cheapness, that must be the final test.

His constructive program did, indeed, look to a transformation of Indian life, by fostering village industries and the better use of the land and the breeding of better and fewer cattle. These, Gandhi held, are among the reforms necessary before large-scale industrialization can be usefully introduced into a country like India, whose capital consists largely of manpower and sunpower. Let man become healthy; let nature be harnessed to the service of man; and then industrial development is due. Even so, it is likely that India will be well advised to avoid the industrial concentration that has disfigured the West. In all this, Gandhi has something to say that all

Asia and Africa, perhaps some parts of Europe and America too, may well ponder. . . .

The constructive program of Gandhi involved the destruction of ancient abuses such as Untouchability. The rich must shed their riches and become trustees or elder brothers to their poor neighbours. Work that involves men in filth and unpleasantness, the work of the *bhangi,* or sweeper, for instance, which has been despised as the most menial, should rather be treated as the most honorable of all professions. Gandhi's economic and social revolution involved, first and foremost, a change of mind, a wholly new attitude towards manual labor, and especially towards the so-called menial tasks. . . .

Perhaps Gandhi is the first important political leader in the world who has consistently kept the needs of the poorest, and above all the voiceless poor of the villages, who are often beyond the sight and the thought of modern social reformers, in the forefront of his mind and heart. To the day of his death, he had them constantly in his mind. He was always at home when he was among them, and he felt imprisoned when he had to dwell in cities. As far as was possible for a man who had to live the life he was called to, and who had travelled about the earth and been educated in London, he identified himself in his every day life with the poorest and the lowliest and the lost. He must abandon everything that he did not strictly need, not because of the spiritual efficacy of asceticism; in the proper sense, Gandhi was not an ascetic. But, so long as one man remained in abject poverty, he held that possession of anything he did not need was a form of theft. Many of his close friends he considered thieves. He tried not to be one himself.

THE CRITICS OF GANDHI

Gandhi and the National Movement: A Marxist View

RAJANI PALME DUTT

Perhaps the sharpest critique of Gandhi's leadership in the Indian national-ist movement was that put forward by Marxists who argued that Gandhi's em-phasis on nonviolence was actually a device for keeping the mass movement from threatening the privileges of the Indian landlords and bourgeoisie, while at the same time utilizing the force of that mass movement as a lever with which to win concessions from India's British rulers. The criticism is manifest throughout the following excerpt from Rajani Palme Dutt's *India Today* (1940). The selection is also important for its presentation of a detailed account of the course of the two campaigns which Gandhi led against the British in 1920–22 and 1930–34, as it mentions many episodes in Gandhi's career which have provoked comment from other critics who do not share Dutt's Marxist approach. Dutt, born in England in 1896 of Indian-Swedish parentage, has been a leading member of the Communist Party of Great Britain since the early 1920's. He is the author of many books, the most recent being *Problems of Contemporary History* (1963). The selection opens with a discussion of the response of the Indian National Congress to the passage of the Montagu-Chelmsford Reforms by the British parliament in 1919.

As late as December, 1919, the Congress still went on record for accept-ance of the [Montagu-Chelmsford] Reforms; but this was only after a sharp di-vision in which Gandhi . . . led the fight for cooperation, while the opposition was led by C. R. Das. . . .[1]

Gandhi's view, as late as the end of 1919, in favor of cooperation and working the Reforms was expressed in an article in his weekly journal at the end of the year:

The Reforms Act coupled with the Proclama-tion is an earnest of the intention of the Brit-ish people to do justice to India and it ought to remove suspicion on that score. . . . Our duty therefore is not to subject the Reforms to carping criticism, but to settle down quietly to work so as to make them a sucess.[2]

This declaration is important, since it was made after the Rowlatt Acts, after Amritsar and martial law in the Punjab — that is, after those issues which are subsequently declared to be the cause of non-cooperation — and thus shows that it was different cal-culations which led to the decision in the following year to inaugurate the non-co-operation movement.

For, in fact, despite the still-continuing cooperation of the Congress, the whole situ-ation in India had changed in 1919, and the basis for cooperation was disappearing

[1] Chitta Ranjan Das (1870–1925), frequently re-ferred to as Deshbandhu ["friend of the coun-try"] Das. [Editor's note]

[2] *Young India,* December 31, 1919.

From Rajani Palme Dutt, *India Today,* 2nd revised edition (Bombay, 1949), pp. 314–329, 332, 334, 337–354. By permission of the author.

from under the feet of the Congress. The year 1919 saw a wave of mass unrest spread over India. Already the closing months of 1918 and the first months of 1919 saw the opening of a strike movement on a scale never before known in India. In December, 1918, the Bombay mill strike began, which by January, 1919, extended to 125,-000 workers. The Rowlatt Acts . . . aroused widespread indignation as demonstrating the iron hand of imperialism beneath the velvet glove of Reform. Gandhi, utilizing his South African experience, sought to organize a passive resistance movement against the Rowlatt Bills, and formed a Satyagraha League for this purpose in February. A *hartal*, or general day of suspension of business, was called for April 6. The response of the masses startled and overwhelmed the initiators of the movement. Through March and April a mighty wave of mass demonstrations, strikes, unrest, in some cases rioting, and courageous resistance to violent repression in the face of heavy casualties, spread over many parts of India. . . . It was at this time that the atrocity of Amritsar occurred. . . .

"The movement," in the view of British official opinion, "assumed the undeniable character of an organized revolt against the British *raj*." [3] Gandhi took alarm at the situation which was developing. In view of sporadic cases of violence of the masses against their rulers which had appeared in Calcutta, Bombay, Ahmedabad and elsewhere, he declared that he had committed "a blunder of Himalayan dimensions which had enabled ill-disposed persons, not true passive resisters at all, to perpetrate disorders." Accordingly, he suspended passive resistance in the middle of April, within a week of the *hartal,* and thus called off the movement at the moment it was beginning to reach its height, on the grounds, as he subsequently explained in a letter to the Press on July 21, that "a civil resister never seeks to embarrass the government." This initial experience of *satyagraha* (literally,

"persistence in truth," used for the method of passive resistance) was to be subsequently repeated on an extended scale.

In December, 1919, as has been seen, the Congress was deciding for working the Reforms, and Gandhi was urging that the task of the national movement was "to settle down quietly to work so as to make them a success." But the situation left no room for such dreams to be realized. The tide of rising mass unrest, which had swept forward in 1919, was still advancing in 1920 and 1921, and was to be further intensified by the economic crisis which began to develop in the latter part of 1920. The first six months of 1920 saw the greatest height of the strike movement, with no less than 200 strikes involving one and a half million workers. Such a rising tide made a mockery of the sage counsels of "settling down quietly." . . .

It was in this situation that in 1920 Gandhi and the main body of the Congress leadership (now deserted by the former Moderates) executed a decisive change of front, threw over cooperation with the Reforms, determined to take the leadership of the rising mass movement and for this purpose evolved the plan of "nonviolent noncooperation." Henceforward the mass struggle was to be led by the Congress; but the price of the leadership was to be that the struggle must be "nonviolent."

The new plan of nonviolent non-cooperation was adopted at the Calcutta Special Congress in September, 1920. It was carried, not without opposition, by the alliance of Gandhi and Motilal Nehru with the militant Muslim leaders, the Ali brothers, at the head of the then powerful Khilafat agitation (in form the protest against the injustices of the Treaty of Sèvres to Turkey, the leading Muslim Power, but in practice the rallying point of Muslim mass unrest). The resolution proclaimed the policy of "progressive nonviolent non-cooperation inaugurated by Mahatma Gandhi, until the said wrongs are righted and *swaraj* is established." . . . The immediate measures were measures of boycott to

* Sir Valentine Chirol, *India*, 1926, p. 207.

be adopted by the middle-class elements, officials, lawyers and students, with the only role for the masses the constructive task of "hand-spinning and hand-weaving"; the active participation of the masses, through nonpayment of taxes (which inevitably meant a No-Rent campaign), was reserved for later.

The boycott of the elections to the new legislatures, which took place in November, was markedly successful, two-thirds of the electors abstaining. The boycott of educational institutions had a considerable measure of success, masses of students sweeping with enthusiasm into the noncooperation movement. The lawyers' boycott was less successful, except for a few outstanding examples, such as those of Motilal Nehru and C. R. Das.

At the annual session of the Congress at Nagpur in December 1920 the new program was finally adopted with practical unanimity. The Creed of the Congress was changed from the previous proclamation of the aim of colonial self-government within the Empire, to be attained by constitutional means, to the new aim of "the attainment of *swaraj* by peaceful and legitimate means." The organization of the Congress was carried forward from its previous loose character to the machinery of a modern party, with its units reaching down to the villages and localities, and with a standing Executive ("Working Committee") of fifteen.

The new program and policy inaugurated by Gandhi marked a giant's advance for the National Congress. The Congress now stood out as a political party leading the masses in struggle against the government for the realisation of national freedom. From this point the National Congress won its position (a position at which the militant nationalists of the earlier years would have rubbed their eyes) as the central focus of the national movement.

But the new program and policy contained also another element, an element alien to the mass struggle, an element of petty-bourgeois moralising speculations and

reformist pacifism, which found its chosen expression in the innocent-seeming term "nonviolent." That term was intended by Gandhi to represent a whole religious-philosophical conception, preached by him with eloquence and devotion, akin in certain respects to older schools of Indian speculative thought, but more closely related to and deriving from late Western schools of thought associated with Tolstoy, Thoreau and Emerson, which had had their vogue and influence during Gandhi's earlier years in the West and in the formation of his thought. That same term was accepted by many of Gandhi's associates, who were far from sharing his philosophical conception, as an apparently common-sense rule of expediency for at any rate the earlier stages of struggle of an unarmed people against a powerfully armed ruling enemy. But in fact, as the subsequent experience of events and the ever-developing interpretation of that term were to demonstrate, that seemingly innocent humanitarian or expedient term contained concealed within it, not only the refusal of the final struggle, but the thwarting also of the immediate struggle by the attempt to conciliate the interests of the masses with the big bourgeois and landlord interests which were inevitably opposed to any decisive mass struggle. Herein lay the contradiction which was to lead to the collapse of the movement, despite great achievements, both in this first trial and in the extended trial a decade later, and the failure to win that speedy victory of *swaraj* which was freely promised as the certain and rapid outcome of the new policy.

A great sweep forward of the mass movement followed the adoption by the Congress of the new militant program of struggle against the government for the speedy realization of *swaraj*. Gandhi freely declared as a firm and certain prophecy (which, despite its naïve character, was confidently believed by his followers in the flush of enthusiasm of those days) the rash promise that *swaraj* would be achieved within twelve months, that is — for the date was definite — by December 31, 1921. He even went so far as to declare, at a conference in September 1921, "that he was so sure of getting *swaraj* before the end of the year that he could not conceive of himself as living beyond December 31 without having won *swaraj*." However, he had still many years of political activity before him, though not yet the fortune of seeing the realization of *swaraj*.

Gandhi's plan of campaign was less clear than the date of victory. The official *History of the Indian National Congress* writes:

Mass civil disobedience was the thing that was luring the people. What was it, what would it be? Gandhi himself never defined it, never elaborated it, never visualized it even to himself. It must unfold itself to a discerning vision, to a pure heart, from step to step, much as the pathway in a dense forest would reveal itself to the wayfarer's feet as he wends his weary way until a ray of light brightens the hopes of an all but despairing wanderer.

Subhas Bose relates his disheartenment when, as an eager young disciple in his first interview with the Mahatma in those fateful days of 1921, he sought to obtain "a clear understanding of the details — the successive stages — of his plan, leading on step by step to the ultimate seizure of power from the foreign bureaucracy," and failed to get an answer:

What his real expectation was, I was unable to understand. Either he did not want to give out all his secrets prematurely or he did not have a clear conception of the tactics whereby the hands of the Government could be forced.

Jawaharlal Nehru writes of the "delightful vagueness" of Gandhi:

It was obvious that to most of our leaders *swaraj* meant something much less than independence. Gandhiji was delightfully vague on the subject, and he did not encourage clear thinking about it either.

However, he explains:

We all felt that he was a great and unique man and a glorious leader, and having put our faith in him we gave him an almost blank cheque, for the time being at least.

The advance of the movement in 1921 was demonstrated, not only in the enthusiastic development of the non-cooperation movement, but in the accompanying rising forms of mass struggle in all parts of the country, as in the Assam-Bengal railway strike, the Midnapore No-Tax campaign, the Moplah rebellion in Malabar in the South, and the militant Akali movement against the government-defended rich Mahants in the Punjab. . . .

By the end of December all the best-known Congress leaders, except Gandhi, were imprisoned. Twenty thousand political prisoners filled the jails. At the highest point of the struggle, at the beginning of the following year, 30,000 were in jail. Enthusiasm was at fever heat.

The government was anxious and perplexed, and began to lose its nerve. If the infection of universal defiance of the government spread from the towns and began to reach the millions of the peasantry, there was no salvation left for British rule; all their guns and aeroplanes would not avail them in the seething cauldron of rebellion of 300 millions. . . .

In this situation the Ahmedabad Congress was held at the close of the year, with Gandhi now almost alone in the leadership. . . .

Amid enthusiasm the Ahmedabad Congress passed resolutions proclaiming "the fixed determination of the Congress to continue the campaign of nonviolent non-cooperation with greater vigor . . . till *swaraj* is established and the control of the government of India passes into the hands of the people," calling on all over eighteen years of age to join the illegal National Volunteers, pledging the aim "to concentrate attention upon civil disobedience, whether mass or individual, whether of an offensive or defensive character," and placing full dictatorial powers for this purpose in the hands of "Mahatma Gandhi as the sole executive authority of the Congress."

Gandhi was now Dictator of the Congress. The movement was at its highest point. Full powers had been placed in his hands to lead it to victory. The moment had come for the final trial of strength, for the launching of mass civil disobedience. The whole country was looking to Gandhi. What would he do?

In the midst of this ferment of national enthusiasm and hope one man on the Congress side was unhappy and alarmed at the development of events. That man was Gandhi. His movement, the movement that he had envisaged, was not developing at all in the way that he had intended. Something was going wrong. This was not the perfect idyllic philosophic "nonviolent" movement he had pictured. He had unchained a monster. Ugly elements were creeping in. Reckless men, especially among his Muslim colleagues, were even beginning to demand the abandonment of the "nonviolence" clause. More and more openly, already in those closing weeks of 1921, when the tens of thousands of fighters were going to prison with his name on their lips, he was expressing his alarm and disgust, as in his revealing cry that *swaraj* stank in his nostrils. . . .

What would Gandhi do? The Ahmedabad Congress had dissolved without a plan. All was left in Gandhi's hands. . . .

Gandhi's action was peculiar. He waited a month. During this month districts approached him, pleading to begin a No-Tax campaign. One district, Guntur, began without permission. Gandhi sent an immediate note to the Congress officials to see that all taxes were paid by the date due. Then he decided to make a beginning with one tiny district where he had taken special care to insure perfect "nonviolent" conditions — the district of Bardoli, with a population of 87,000 — or one four-thousandth part of the Indian people that was awaiting his leadership to act. On February 1 he sent his ultimatum to the Viceroy to declare that, unless the prisoners were re-

leased and repressive measures abandoned, "mass civil disobedience" would begin — in Bardoli exclusively. Hardly had he done this when, a few days later, news arrived that at a little village, Chauri Chaura in the United Provinces, angry peasants had stormed and burned the village police station resulting in the death of twenty-two policemen. This news of the growth of unrest among the peasantry immediately determined Gandhi that there was no time to be lost. At a hasty meeting of the Working Committee at Bardoli on February 12, the decision was reached, in view of the "inhuman conduct of the mob at Chauri Chaura," to end, not only mass civil disobedience, but the whole campaign of civil disobedience through volunteer processions, the holding of public meetings under ban and the like, and to substitute a "constructive" program of spinning, temperance reform and educational activities. The battle was over. The whole campaign was over. The mountain had indeed borne a mouse.

To say that the Bardoli decision created consternation in the Congress camp would be to fall short of any power of language to describe the feelings that were aroused. . . .

To sound the order of retreat just when public enthusiasm was reaching the boiling point was nothing short of a national calamity. The principal lieutenants of the Mahatma, Deshbandhu Das, Pandit Motilal Nehru and Lala Lajpat Rai, who were all in prison, shared the popular resentment. I was with the Deshbandhu at the time, and I could see that he was beside himself with anger and sorrow.[4]

Motilal Nehru, Lajpat Rai and others sent from prison long and indignant letters to Gandhi protesting at his decision. Gandhi coldly replied that men in prison were "civilly dead" and had no claim to any say in policy.

The entire movement, which had been organised on the basis of complete discouragement of any spontaneous mass activity

[4] Subhas Bose, *The Indian Struggle*, p. 90.

and mechanical subordination to the will of one man, was inevitably thrown into helpless confusion and demoralization by the Bardoli decision. . . .

After the movement had been thus paralysed and demoralised from within, the government struck with confidence. On March 10 Gandhi was arrested and sentenced to six years' imprisonment. Not a ripple followed in the mass movement. Within less than two years Gandhi was released. The crisis was over.

Great controversy has raged over the Bardoli decision and its bitter consequences for the national movement in the six years' subsequent ebb that followed. Defenses have been put forward that the real cause and justification of the decision must be sought deeper than in the alleged issue of Chauri Chaura, officially given as the reason for the decision, and that in reality the time had come when it was essential to stop the movement because "our movement, in spite of its apparent power and widespread enthusiasm, was going to pieces."[5] It may be asked in what sense the movement was "going to pieces." If by this is meant that the reformist-pacifist control of the movement was weakening, this is undoubtedly correct. But this advance was inherent in the advance of the movement and the condition of its future victory (Nehru's assumption of the inevitability of the government's victory in the face of an all-Indian popular revolt would not have been as cheerfully assumed by the government). If, on the other hand, it might be taken to mean that the effective strength of the mass struggle had in reality passed its highest point and was weakening, such a claim would certainly not be correct, and is, indeed, not intended to be suggested even by the apologists. The clearest evidence of this is afforded by the government's own grave estimate of the actual forces of the situation three days before the Bardoli collapse. On February 9, 1922, the Viceroy telegraphed to London:

The lower classes in the towns have been seriously affected by the non-cooperation movement, . . . In certain areas the peasantry have been affected, particularly in parts of the Assam Valley, United Provinces, Bihar and Orissa and Bengal. As regards the Punjab, the Akali agitation . . . has penetrated to the rural Sikhs. A large proportion of the Mohammedan population throughout the country are embittered and sullen . . . grave possibilities. . . . The Governnment of India are prepared for disorder of a more formidable nature than has in the past occurred, and do not seek to minimize in any way the fact that great anxiety is caused by the situation.[6]

This was the government's picture of the situation three days before the whole campaign was cancelled by the Bardoli decision on February 12.[7]

The discipline of the mass movement and readiness for decisive struggle were shown by the example of Guntur, where, in despite of Gandhi's orders, through a misunderstanding the No-Tax campaign was inaugurated. Not five per cent of the taxes were collected — until Gandhi's countermanding order came. On a word of command from the Congress center this process could have undoubtedly been unleashed throughout the country, and would have turned into a universal refusal of land revenue and rent. But this process would have meant the sweeping away, not only of imperialism, but also of landlordism.

[6] *Telegraphic Correspondence Regarding the Situation in India,* Cmd. 1586, 1922.
[7] The impression of the Government on the crisis of 1922 and their view that only Gandhi's calling off of the movement saved them was subsequently expressed by Lord Lloyd, then Governor of Bombay, in an interview:

"He gave us a scare! His program filled our jails. You can't go on arresting people forever, you know — not when there are 319,000,000 of them. And if they had taken his next step and refused to pay taxes! God knows where we should have been!

"Gandhi's was the most colossal experiment in world history; and it came within an inch of succeeding. But he couldn't control men's passions. They became violent and he called off his program. You know the rest. We jailed him." [Lord Lloyd in an interview with Drew Pearson, quoted by C. F. Andrews in the *New Republic*, April 3, 1939.]

[5] Nehru, *Autobiography*, p. 85.

That these considerations were the decisive considerations behind the Bardoli decision is proved by the text of the decision itself. The text of the resolution adopted by the Working Committee at Bardoli on February 12 is so important as to deserve reproduction, and repays careful study for the light it throws on the forces and contradictions of the Indian national movement. The essential clauses run:

Clause 1. The Working Committee deplores the inhuman conduct of the mob at Chauri Chaura in having brutally murdered constables and wantonly burned police *thana* (station).

Clause 2. In view of the violent outbreaks every time mass civil disobedience is inaugurated, indicating that the country is not nonviolent enough, the Working Committee of the Congress resolves that mass civil disobedience . . . be suspended, and *instructs the local Congress Committees to advise the cultivators to pay land revenue and other taxes due to the government,* and to suspend every other activity of an offensive character.

Clause 3. The suspension of mass civil disobedience shall be continued until the atmosphere is so nonviolent as to ensure the nonrepetition of atrocities such as Gorakhpur or of the hooliganism such as at Bombay and Madras on the 17th of November and the 13th of January. . . .

Clause 5. All volunteer processions and public meetings for the defiance of authority should be stopped.

Clause 6. The Working Committee advises Congress workers and organizations to inform the ryots (peasants) that withholding of rent payment to the zemindars (landlords) is contrary to the Congress resolutions and injurious to the best interests of the country.

Clause 7. The Working Committee assures the zemindars that the Congress movement is in no way intended to attack their legal rights, and that even where the ryots have grievances, the Committee desires that redress be sought by mutual consultation and arbitration.

The resolution shows that it was not an abstract question of nonviolence which actuated the movers. It will be noted that no less than three clauses (italicised) deal specifically, emphatically and even urgently with the necessity of the *payment of rent* by the peasants to the landlords or government. There is here no question of violence or nonviolence. There is simply a question of class interests, of exploiters and exploited. The nonpayment of rent could not be suggested by any one to be a "violent" action: on the contrary, it is a most peaceful (though also most revolutionary) form of protest. Why, then, should a resolution, nominally condemning "violence," concentrate so emphatically on this question of the nonpayment of rent and the "legal rights" of landlords? There is only one answer possible. The phraseology of "nonviolence" is revealed as only in reality a cover, conscious or unconscious, for class interests and the maintenance of class exploitation.

The dominant leadership of the Congress associated with Gandhi called off the movement because they were afraid of the awakening mass activity; and they were afraid of the mass activity because it was beginning to threaten those propertied class interests with which they themselves were still in fact closely linked.

Not the question of "violence" or "nonviolence," but the question of class interest in opposition to the mass movement, was the breaking-point of the national struggle in 1922. This was the rock on which the movement broke. This was the real meaning of "nonviolence."

For half a decade after the blow of Bardoli the national movement was prostrated.

*   *   *

Towards the end of 1927 the Simon Commission was announced, to settle the fate of the future constitution for India, with a complete exclusion of Indian representation.

Thus the Indian bourgeoisie, however unwillingly, found themselves once again forced to turn aside from their hopes of cooperation and to look towards the possibility of harnessing the mass forces once more in their support, if they were to have any prospect of driving a successful bargain. But the conditions were now far more difficult and complicated than a decade ago. For in the interval the mass forces had begun to awaken to new life of their own, to independent political expression and aims, and to active struggle, not only against imperialism, but against the Indian exploiters. The triangular character of the contest, or rather the deeper contest between imperialism and the Indian masses, with the hesitant and vacillating role of the Indian bourgeoisie, was now coming far more clearly to the front. Hence the peculiar character of the new stage of struggle which now opened out, developing from its first signs in the latter part of 1927 to its full strength in 1930–34: on the one hand, the far more widespread, intensive and prolonged character of the struggle; on the other, the spasmodic, interrupted tempo of development, the zigzag vacillation of aims, the repeated accompanying negotiations, and sudden truces without settlement, until the final collapse.

*   *   *

In this critical balance of forces, with the certainty of big new struggles ahead in a far more advanced situation than a decade previously, the right-wing leadership once again turned to Gandhi, whom they had previously thrust aside, and whose star now once again rose. At the Calcutta session at the end of 1928 Gandhi returned to active leadership of the Congress. Whatever the views of the moderate leaders might be with regard to his personal idiosyncrasies, there was no question that he was the most subtle and experienced politician of the older group, with unrivalled mass prestige which world publicity had now enhanced as the greatest Indian figure; the ascetic defender of property in the name of the most religious and idealist principles of humility and love of poverty; the invincible metaphysical-theological casuist who could justify and reconcile anything and everything in an astounding tangle of explanations and arguments

which in a man of common clay might have been called dishonest quibbling, but in the great ones of the earth like [the Labour Party prime minister] MacDonald or Gandhi is recognized as a higher plane of spiritual reasoning; the prophet who by his personal saintliness and selflessness could unlock the door to the hearts of the masses where the moderate bourgeois leaders could not hope for a hearing — and the best guarantee of the shipwreck of any mass movement which had the blessing of his association. This Jonah of revolution, this general of unbroken disasters was the mascot of the bourgeoisie in each wave of the developing Indian struggle. So appeared once again the characteristic feature of modern Indian politics, the unwritten article of every successive Indian constitution — the indispensability of Gandhi (actually the expression of the precarious balance of class forces). All the hopes of the bourgeoisie (the hostile might say, the hopes of imperialism) were fixed on Gandhi as the man to ride the waves, to unleash just enough of the mass movement in order to drive a successful bargain, and at the same time to save India from revolution.

*   *   *

At the Lahore Congress . . . at the end of 1929 the decision for action was taken. The Nehru Report, embodying Dominion Status, was declared to have lapsed and *Purna Swaraj* or Complete Independence was adopted as henceforth the Creed of the Congress. The Congress authorized the All-India Congress Committee "whenever it deems fit, to launch upon a program of civil disobedience, including nonpayment of taxes. . . ." On January 26, 1930, the first Independence Day was celebrated throughout India in vast demonstrations at which the pledge to struggle for complete independence was read out, proclaiming it "a crime against man and God to submit any longer" to British rule, and declaring the conviction that "if we can but withdraw our voluntary help and stop payment of taxes, without doing violence even under provocation, the end of this inhuman rule is assured."

What was to be the aim of the struggle that now opened? What was to be the plan of campaign? What were to be the minimum conditions which would be regarded as justifying a settlement? In what way was such irresistible pressure to be brought on the British government as to compel "the end of this inhuman rule?" On all these questions there was from the outset no clearness.

Complete independence might appear to have been the defined aim of the campaign, and was probably so regarded by the majority of the Congress membership and by the masses who responded to the Congress call. Indeed, the recorded last dying words of Motilal Nehru, who died on the eve of the Irwin-Gandhi Agreement, appear to suggest that this had been his conception of the struggle:

Let me die, if die I must, in the lap of a free India. Let me sleep my last sleep, not in a subject country, but in a free one.

This was not, however, the conception of Gandhi. Immediately after Lahore he published a statement, through the *New York World* of January 9, that "the independence resolution need frighten nobody" (repeated in his letter to the Viceroy in March), and on January 30, through his paper *Young India,* he made an offer of Eleven Points, covering various reforms (rupee ratio of 1s. 4d., total prohibition, reduction of land revenue and military expenditure, protective tariff on foreign cloth, etc.) in return for which civil disobedience would be called off. The publication of the Eleven Points on the eve of the struggle served to intimate to the other side that the claim for independence was to be regarded as only a bargaining counter, a kind of conventional maximum at the opening of a traditional bazar haggling, which could be placed on one side in return for substantial concession.

The strategy of the campaign was equally unclear. Once again the Congress Committee meeting at Sabarmati in February 1930 placed power in the hands of "Mahatma Gandhi and those working with him" (not any elected organ of the Congress) to lead and control the campaign, on the grounds that "civil disobedience must be initiated and controlled by those who believe in nonviolence . . . *as an article of faith.*" But what were to be the lines of the campaign which was thus handed over without directives from the elected Congress leadership? Subhas Bose writes, referring to the Lahore Congress:

On behalf of the left wing a resolution was moved, by the writer, to the effect that the Congress should aim at setting up a parallel government in the country, and to that end should take up the task of organizing the workers, peasants and youths. This resolution was defeated, with the result that though the Congress accepted the goal of complete independence as its objective, no plan was laid down for reaching that goal — nor was any program of work adopted for the coming year. A more ridiculous state of affairs could not be imagined.

*   *   *

The official Congress History rebukes those who demanded to know the plan of campaign:

Those gathered at Sabarmati inquired of Gandhi about his plans. It was but right that they should do so, although nobody would have asked Lord Kitchener or Marshal Foch or von Hindenburg to unfold their plans on the eve of the Great War. Plans they had, but they might not reveal them. It was not so with Satyagraha. There was no privacy about our plans. But they were not clear-cut either. They would unfold themselves, much as the path on a misty morning reveals itself to a fast-moving motor, almost from yard to yard. The Satyagrahi carried a searchlight on his forehead. It shows the way for the next step.

Everything thus depended on Gandhi's conception of the campaign. The country and its fortunes were handed over to his guidance.

It is evident that two opposing conceptions of the campaign were possible, according to the conception of the aim. Either it was to be a decisive struggle of all the forces of the Indian people for the ending of British rule and the establishment of complete independence . . . or it was intended to be a limited and regulated demonstration of mass pressure with a view to securing better terms and concessions from British rule. The former was clearly the conception of the Lahore Congress, and what the masses of the people in India were expecting. But if this were the aim, to undertake so gigantic a task and reduce to impotence a formidable opponent, it is evident that any hope of success depended on rapidly throwing the maximum forces into the offensive with a view to overwhelming the opposing forces before any effective countermeasures could be taken: the calling of a General Strike, with the entire weight of the Congress and working-class movement behind it, the calling of the entire peasantry to a No-Tax and No-Rent campaign, and the setting up of a parallel national government with its organs, courts, Volunteer Corps, etc., throughout the country. Such a campaign, in the then heightened state of national and mass feeling, could have, if conducted with extreme speed and resoluteness, stood a reasonable chance of mobilising the mass of the people, isolating imperialism (the Garhwali mutiny, and the experience of Peshawar and Sholapur showed the great possibilities of this), and winning independence.

This was not the conception of Gandhi. Indeed, it is clear from all his expressions at the time and after that his main problem was how to prevent such a development of the struggle. In an article in May 1931 he explained that he preferred defeat to victory if the price of victory should be infringement "by a hair's breadth" of his doctrine of nonviolence:

I would welcome even utter failure with nonviolence unimpaired, rather than depart from it by a hair's breadth to achieve a doubtful success.

In his letter to the Viceroy in March 1930 Gandhi made clear his analysis of the forces underlying the struggle, and his purpose in undertaking its leadership:

The party of violence is gaining ground and making itself felt. . . . It is my purpose to set in motion that force (nonviolence) as well against the organized violence force of the British rule as the unorganised violence force of the growing party of violence. To sit still would be to give rein to both the forces above mentioned.

Thus on the eve of rising mass struggle Gandhi proclaimed the fight on two fronts, not only against British rule, but against the internal enemy in India. This conception of the fight on two fronts corresponds to the role of the Indian bourgeoisie, alarmed as it sees the ground sinking beneath its feet with the growing conflict of imperialism and the mass movement, compelled to undertake leadership of the struggle, despite the "mad risk" (in Gandhi's phrase in his letter to the Viceroy), in order to hold it within bounds ("to sit still would be to give rein to both the forces above mentioned"), and seeking to conciliate both with the magic wand of "nonviolence." However, "nonviolence" . . . was *one-way nonviolence.*" It was "nonviolence" for the Indian masses, but not for imperialism, which practised violence to its heart's content — and won the battle.

Gandhi's strategy corresponded to this conception of the struggle. Given this understanding, that it was not a strategy intended to lead to the victory of independence, but to find the means in the midst of a formidable revolutionary wave to maintain leadership of the mass movement and yet place the maximum bounds and restraints upon it, it was a skillful and able strategy. This was shown already in his brilliant choice of the first objective of the campaign and the method of conducting it. He decided to lead the fight against the salt monopoly of the government. This diverted the fight from the possibility of participation by the industrial working class, the one force which Gandhi has made clear in every utterance that he fears in India; it was capable of enlisting the support and popular interest of the peasantry, while diverting them from any struggle against the landlords. To make assurance doubly sure, Gandhi intended at first to confine the campaign to himself and a small band of chosen disciples:

So far as I am concerned, my intention is to start the movement only through the inmates of the Ashrama and those who have submitted to its discipline and assimilated its methods.

So followed the march to Dandi, on the seashore, by Gandhi and his seventy-eight hand-picked followers, dragging on through three precious weeks, with the newsreel cameras of the world clicking away, while the masses were called on to wait expectant. The enormous publicity which was given to this Salt March through the press, the cinema and every other device, was regarded by the Congress leadership as a triumph of strategy for awakening and mobilising the masses; but, while it is undoubtedly true that it did help to perform this function for the more backward elements among the masses, the free encouragement and permission given by the imperialist authorities for this publicity, in striking contrast to their later attitude (and to their very alert arrest of Subhas Bose, the leading left nationalist, even before Independence Day, before the struggle opened), was evidently not simple naïveté and failure to understand its significance, but, on the contrary, very sharp understanding of its significance and direct help to ensure the diversion of the mass movement into the channels which were being prepared for it by Gandhi.

Nevertheless, the moment the three weeks were completed with the ceremonial boiling of salt by Gandhi on the seashore on April 6 (not followed by arrest), the overwhelming mass movement which broke loose throughout the country took the leadership on both sides by surprise. The official instructions given were confined to the most limited and relatively harmless forms of civil disobedience: violation of the Salt Law, boycott of foreign cloth, picketing of the foreign cloth shops and government liquor shops. Gandhi's conception of the movement was shown in the instructions given by him on April 9:

Our path has already been chalked out for us. Let every village fetch or manufacture contraband salt, sisters should picket liquor shops, opium dens and foreign cloth dealers' shops. Young and old in every home should ply the *takli* [spindle] and spin and get woven heaps of yarn every day. Foreign cloth should be burnt. Hindus should eschew untouchability. Hindus, Mussulmans, Sikhs, Parsis and Christians should all achieve heart unity. Let the majority rest content with what remains after the minorities have been satisfied. Let students leave government schools and colleges, and government servants resign their service and devote themselves to the service of the people, and we shall soon find that *Purna Swaraj* will come knocking at our doors.

The mass movement which developed already in April went considerably beyond these simple limits, with rising strikes, powerful mass demonstrations, the Chittagong Armoury Raid in Bengal, the incidents at Peshawar, which was in the hands of the people for ten days, and the beginnings of spontaneous No-Rent movements by the peasants in a number of localities, especially in the United Provinces, where the Congress vainly sought to mediate on a basis of 50 per cent payment of rents.

Most significant for the whole future was the refusal of the Garhwali soldiers at Peshawar to fire on the people. Following the arrest of local leaders, armored cars were sent to cow the angry mass demonstrations; one armored car was burned, its occupants escaping; thereupon wholesale firing on the crowds was followed by hundreds of deaths and casualties. Two platoons of the Second Battalion of the 18th Royal Garhwali Rifles, Hindu troops in the midst of a Muslim crowd, refused the order to fire, broke ranks, fraternized with the crowd, and a number handed over their arms. Immediately after this, the military and police were completely withdrawn from Peshawar; from April 25 to May 4 the city was in the hands of the people, until powerful British forces, with air squadrons, were concentrated to "recapture" Peshawar; there was no resistance. The government subsequently refused all demands for an enquiry into the incident. Seventeen men of the Garhwali Rifles were subjected by court-martial to savage sentences, one to transportation for life, one to fifteen years' rigorous imprisonment, and fifteen to terms varying from three to ten years.

The example of the Garhwali soldiers, who refused to fire upon their fellow-countrymen, might have been thought, to put it at its lowest, at least a triumphant demonstration of "nonviolence," which should have been dear to the heart of Gandhi. This was not, however, Gandhi's view. This was a nonviolence which really threatened the foundations of British rule. In the Irwin-Gandhi Agreement the clause for the release of prisoners specifically excluded the Garhwali men. . . . Gandhi subsequently explained to a French interviewer, during his visit to the Round Table Conference in London, his reasons for disapproving of the Garhwali men:

A soldier who disobeys an order to fire breaks the oath which he has taken and renders himself guilty of criminal disobedience. I cannot ask officials and soldiers to disobey; for when I am in power, I shall in all likelihood make use of those same officials and those same soldiers. If I taught them to disobey I should be afraid that they might do the same when I am in power.[8]

This sentence (which may be recommended to the study of every pacifist admirer of Gandhi), no less clearly than the

previous Bardoli decision, throws a flood of light on the real meaning of "nonviolence."

When it became clear that the power of the mass movement was exceeding the limits set it, and that the authority of Gandhi, who had been left at liberty, was in danger of waning, on May 5 the government arrested Gandhi. . . .

The response to the arrest was shown in the wave of *hartals* and mass strikes all over India. In the industrial town of Sholapur in the Bombay Presidency, with 140,-000 inhabitants, of whom 50,000 were textile operatives, the workers held possession of the town for a week, replacing the police and establishing their own administration, until martial law was proclaimed on May 12. . . .

Imperialist repression was limitless. Ordinances followed one another in rapid succession, creating a situation comparable to martial law. In June the Congress and all its organizations were declared illegal. Official figures recorded 60,000 civil resisters sentenced in less than a year up to the Irwin-Gandhi Agreement in the spring of 1931. These figures are certainly an underestimate. . . .

Imprisonment was the least of the forms of repression. The jails were filled to overflowing, and it was clear that wholesale imprisonment was powerless to check the movement. Therefore the principal weapon employed was physical terrorism. The records of indiscriminate *lathi*[9] charges, beating up, firing on unarmed crowds, killing and wounding of men and women, and punitive expeditions made an ugly picture. The strictest measures were employed to cast a veil of censorship over the whole proceedings; but the careful records of the Congress provide volumes of certified and attested facts and incidents which throw some light on the brutality employed.

Nevertheless, the power of the movement during 1930, exceeding every calculation of the authorities, and growing in

[8] Reply to the French journalist Charles Petrasch on the question of the Garhwali soldiers, *Monde*, February 20, 1932.

[9] A long metal-tipped wood or bamboo staff, used by police in India. [Editor's note]

spite of repression, began to raise the most serious alarm in the imperialist camp, which already found open expression by the summer of 1930, especially in the British trading community, who were hard hit by the boycott. This was especially noticeable in Bombay, where was the center of strength of the industrial working class, where repression was most severe, but where the movement was strongest, and again and again held possession of the streets, despite repeated police charges, in mass demonstrations which the Congress leaders vainly begged to disperse, and in which the red flags were conspicuous beside the Congress flags, or even predominated. . . . The British businessmen in Bombay joined with the Indian businessmen, through the Millowners' Association (with a one-third European element) and the Chamber of Commerce, in demanding immediate self-government for India on a Dominion basis. The amazing spectacle was witnessed of the *Times of India* (Bombay) clamouring for responsible parliamentary government at the center. . . .

Thus a situation of "defeatism" and "demoralization" bordering on panic, despite all the bluster and repression, was beginning to show itself in the imperialist camp; and it became essential for imperialism at all costs to negotiate a settlement. On the basis of the struggle and sacrifices of the Indian people the Congress leadership held a strong hand. The only hopes of imperialism for salvation were now placed in the moderate national leadership, whose alarm at the extension and unknown possibilities of the mass struggle they knew to be genuine. After an interview with Gandhi in September, Professor H. G. Alexander, Professor of International Relations at Selly Oak College, Birmingham, reported the views of Gandhi:

Even in the seclusion of his prison he is acutely conscious that such embitterment is developing, and for that reason he would welcome a return to peace and cooperation as soon as it could be honestly obtained. . . .

His influence is still great, but more dangerous and uncontrollable forces are gathering strength daily.

Thus the alarm grew on both sides; and on the basis of this mutual alarm there was the possibility of a settlement — against the Indian people. . . .

On January 26 Gandhi and the Congress Working Committee were released unconditionally and given freedom to meet. Gandhi declared that he left prison with "an absolutely open mind." Prolonged negotiations followed. On March 4 the Irwin-Gandhi Agreement was signed, and the struggle was declared provisionally suspended.

The Irwin-Gandhi Agreement secured not a single aim of the Congress struggle (not even the repeal of the Salt Tax). Civil disobedience was to be withdrawn. Congress was to participate in the Round Table Conference, which it had sworn to boycott. Not a single concrete step to self-government was granted. . . .

The fact that the British government had been compelled to sign a public treaty with the leader of the National Congress, which it had previously declared an unlawful association and sought to smash, was undoubtedly a tremendous demonstration of the strength of the national movement. This fact produced at first a widespread sense of elation and victory, except among the more politically conscious sections, who understood what had happened and saw that all the struggle and sacrifice had been thrown away at the negotiating table. Only slowly, as the meaning of the terms began to be understood, the realization dawned that nothing whatever had been gained. All the aims of complete independence and no compromise with imperialism, so loudly proclaimed at Lahore, had gone up in smoke. Even Gandhi's Eleven Points, which had previously been an offer of a compromise surrender behind the back of the Congress, had now vanished; not one had been conceded. The Congress was now reduced to accepting the Round Table

Conference, which it had previously refused, and in which it could have participated anyway without a struggle (save that it could have obtained far better representation, had it chosen to demand this at the start).

The Irwin-Gandhi Agreement thus repeated the Bardoli experience on an enlarged scale. Once again the movement was suddenly and mysteriously called off at the moment when it was reaching its height ("The suggestion of the impending collapse of our movement is entirely false; the movement was showing no signs of slackening," [said] Gandhi [in an] interview to *Monde,* February 20, 1932, on the situation at the time of the Agreement). "Such a victory has seldom been vouchsafed to any Viceroy," jubilated *The Times* on March 5. "The Congress has never made any bid for victory," explained Gandhi in his statement to the astonished pressmen on March 5 justifying the Agreement, and in this respect expressing certainly the truth of his strategy. Later, he explained his thought further. "We should give up the attempt to secure a *Swaraj* Constitution at the present moment," he wrote in *Young India* in June, 1931; "we can gain our end without political power." Alternatively, he explained, in an interview to the Press on March 6, that *Purna Swaraj* really means "disciplined self-rule from within" and by no means excludes "association with England" ("association" is delicate — especially when it means "association" with the sharp end of a bayonet). So the phrases were poured out, by Gandhi on the one side as by MacDonald on the other, to confuse the plain aim of independence as proclaimed at Lahore ("complete freedom from British domination and British imperialism") in a wealth of legal interpretation and theological casuistry, until it was difficult to know whether to award the palm to Gandhi or to MacDonald, both masters of the art of the bewildering phrase and the higher spiritual appeal to conceal the realities of capitulation and slavery.

The Karachi Congress, hastily convened

the same month, unanimously endorsed the Agreement. Jawaharlal Nehru was given the task of moving it, "not without great mental conflict and physical distress." "Was it for this," he thought, "that our people had behaved so gallantly for a year? Were all our brave words and deeds to end in this?" He felt, however, that it would only be "personal vanity" to express his dissent. . . .

Outside the Congress, sharp criticism of the Agreement was expressed from the youth and from the working-class movement. . . .

Disillusionment rapidly spread to wider circles. The role of Gandhi at the Round Table Conference in London during 1931 (and among the devotees of higher ethical thought in England who crowded round him in the intervals in innumerable little receptions and gatherings to hear the message of the World Teacher) was an unhappy farce, over which a veil is best drawn. The honor of the Congress was lowered by its inclusion as an item in this motley array of government puppets brought like captives to imperial Rome to display their confusion and division for the amusement of Westminster legislators. Gandhi returned, meeting Mussolini on the way. He brought back no fruits from the Round Table Conference.

On his way back Gandhi expressed the hope that there would be no need to renew the struggle; from Port Said he cabled the India Office that he would do all in his power for peace. He drafted a resolution to this effect immediately on return. But he reckoned without his host.

Imperialism, once it had secured the whip-hand, was determined to use its advantage to the utmost. The "truce" from the outset had been one-sided; repression had continued. Gandhi returned in the last days of 1931 to hear a pitiful tale from his colleagues. He cabled at once to the Viceroy, begging for an interview. It was refused. Imperialism had utilized every day of that nine months' truce (while the comedy had been enacted in London) to complete its grim preparations for a decisive battle. . . .

Swift and sharp the blow fell on January 4, 1932. On the same day negotiations were broken; the Viceroy issued his Manifesto; Gandhi was arrested; Ordinances appeared in a batch (no dribbling out this time, one by one, as they were thought of, as in 1930, but straight from the pigeon-holes on the first day); all the principal Congress leaders and organizers were arrested all over the country; the Congress and all its organizations were declared illegal, their press banned, their premises, funds and property confiscated. A triumph of organization. . . .

The Congress leadership was taken by surprise. This was such a sudden change from the atmosphere of the Round Table Conference. They had made no preparations. In 1930 the Congress had been on the offensive. Now it was thrown on the defensive. They had not realized the price of the Irwin-Gandhi Agreement. . . .

The government had counted on a fight to a finish in six weeks. The toughness of the national movement was such that the battle, despite the unfavourable conditions, dragged on for twenty-nine months before the final surrender. But it was a soldiers' battle without strategic leadership. Under the conditions of illegality and violent repression the task of leadership was in any case sufficiently difficult. But it was not rendered easier by the actions of Gandhi and the High Command, whose role amounted, not merely to abdication, but to repudiation of leadership. Orders were actually issued against secrecy (under illegal conditions!) as a perversion of Congress principles. A resolution was issued to the zamindars (landlords) to assure them that no campaign would be approved against their interests. By the summer of 1932 Gandhi abandoned all public interest in the national struggle, and devoted himself to the cause of the Harijans (untouchables). His dramatic "fast unto death" in September was directed, not against the

repression, not to any object of the life-and-death struggle of the national movement going on, but to prevent the scheme of separate representation for the "depressed classes." It ended, neither in death nor in the attainment of its objective, but in the Poona Pact, by which the number of reserved seats for the "depressed classes" was doubled. The episode served to divert attention from the national struggle, of which he was still supposed to be the responsible leader.

In May 1933 Gandhi began a new fast, directed, not against the government, but to change the heart of his countrymen. He described it as a "heart-prayer for purification of myself and my associates for greater vigilance and watchfulness in connection with the Harijan cause." The delighted government released him unconditionally. . . .

It was not until May, 1934, that the final end came to the struggle which had opened with such magnificent power in 1930. In April Gandhi had issued a statement explaining his view of the reasons for the failure of the movement. The fault lay with the masses.

I feel that the masses have not yet received the message of satyagraha owing to its adulteration in the process of transmission. It has become clear to me that spiritual instruments suffer in their potency when their use is taught through non-spiritual media. . . . The indifferent civil resistance of many . . . has not touched the hearts of the rulers.

Even the transition from mass civil disobedience to individual civil disobedience had not solved this problem of the uncontrollable character of any mass movement. The conclusion was drawn with faultless logic.

Satyagraha needs to be confined to one qualified person at a time. In the present circumstances only one, and that myself, should for the time being bear the responsibility of civil disobedience.

Such was the final *reductio ad absurdum* of the Gandhist theory of "nonviolent non-cooperation" as the path of liberation for the Indian people.

In May 1934 the All-India Congress Committee was allowed to meet at Patna to end civil disobedience unconditionally (with the solitary exception recommended by Gandhi). There were no terms and no concessions from the government. . . .

In the autumn of 1934 Gandhi resigned from membership of the Congress, his work for the time being accomplished. In a parting statement he explained that "there is a growing and vital difference of outlook between many Congressmen and myself." It was clear that for "the majority of Congressmen" nonviolence was not "a fundamental creed," but only "a policy." Socialist groups were growing in the Congress in numbers and influence: "if they gain ascendancy in the Congress, as they well may, I cannot remain in the Congress." The new stage was making itself felt; and it was unwelcome to the old ideas.

Gandhi left the Congress. But he did not leave until he had bequeathed to it a reactionary revision of its Constitution and organization, which considerably hampered its further progressive development. And he remained the most powerful guiding influence behind the scenes, ready in case of need to assume direct leadership anew. In the crisis of 1939–40 and again in 1942 he assumed direct leadership.

Gandhi and the Congress: A Muslim View

K. SARWAR HASAN

Most Pakistani writers have been too preoccupied with tracing the Islamic background of their own new nation to devote much attention to Gandhi's role in the history of India prior to independence and partition. However, this brief excerpt from a study of *The Genesis of Pakistan*, published in 1950, makes clear some of the reasons why Gandhi never succeeded in attracting as wide a following among Muslims as he did in his own religious community. The author is secretary of the Pakistan Institute of International Affairs.

IN 1919, there was widespread anger against the British, generally because of the conservative character of the proposed constitutional reforms and the Amritsar massacres and, amongst the Muslims, on account of the terms of the Treaty of Sèvres, which, in violation of solemn pledges, threatened to dismember Turkey. All sections of the people were in ferment. Mohandas Karamchand Gandhi, consolidating their joint and several grievances, proposed that the Congress should launch a campaign of mass non-cooperation with the British rule. Almost all the senior leaders of the Congress declared themselves against this course. But they would have been left high and dry, if they had persisted in their opposition, for the Mahatma had captured the imagination of the masses. With characteristic courage, Jinnah, who

From K. Sarwar Hasan, *The Genesis of Pakistan* (Karachi, 1950), pp. 9–12, 17–18. By permission of the author.

had in his earlier days defied the Muslim community by joining the Congress, now risked political exile from the Congress, at a time when he was one of its front rank leaders, by publicly opposing Gandhi's desperate proposals. Jinnah's intellectual honesty made it impossible for him to follow Gandhi, whose belief in "soul force" and in his "inner voice" and whose devotion to the cow, were anathema to him. Gandhi talked in mystic metaphors and apparently wished to banish modern science and institutions from India, and advocated a return to a mediaeval society. Jinnah felt that Gandhi's methods of forcing the political pace of the country would plunge it into turmoil and widen the gap between the Muslims and the Hindus. Jinnah evidently believed with Gokhale in the need for "peace and order which were necessary for slowly evolving a nation out of heterogeneous elements of which India was composed."

Indeed Gandhi, while he pleaded for Hindu-Muslim unity, at various times, with varying degrees of emphasis, by his personal conduct and public activities, emphasised the heterogeneous character of the elements of which India was composed. He rejected the approach of the earlier leaders of the Congress, who, drawing their inspiration from the West, sought to build a nation on entirely secular lines. The life, manners and speech of Gandhi were those of a Hindu par excellence, indeed, a self-abnegating Hindu — a Mahatma — who, according to Hindu religious tradition, should be held in reverence. He drew his inspiration principally from the Hindu holy book, the Gita. He talked of Indian independence as *Ram Raj,* the rule of the Hindu god, Rama; the struggle for it was to him *dharma yudh*, which to anyone would mean Hindu religious war. . . .

Gandhi did not attack, or ask for the liquidation of, the Hindu system of caste as the supreme barrier between the Hindus and the Muslims. The fundamental assumption of Hindu social organisation is

that a man is born — must be born — in one of the four castes and must remain in it and die in it. None can enter the fold; none can get out of it. It is strange that Gandhi did not realize that it was this institutional exclusiveness that militated against the Hindus as a whole having fellow-feeling for the Muslims or the Untouchables, whose cause he publicly espoused.

None of these things was calculated permanently to endear Gandhi's movement to the Muslims. Following the turmoil, riots broke out between Hindus and Muslims, for which important Hindu Congress leaders, the entire Hindu press, and even Gandhi, put the blame on the Muslims. The Hindu *Mahasabha* now emerged as the exponent of militant Hinduism, publicly demanding the virtual suppression of the Muslims. Many of its leaders were close personal friends of Gandhi and were important leaders of the Congress also.

But the most disconcerting fact for the Muslims was that the Hindu community as a body, including almost all the rank and file of the Congress, was becoming hostile to the principle of separate electorates, which was the basis of the Lucknow Pact [of 1916, between the Congress and the Muslim League —].

*   *   *

In 1930, Gandhi launched his second mass movement, which a year later, he interrupted to attend the London Round Table Conference between British and Indian leaders. At this Conference, Jinnah, still not disillusioned, achieved what might be described as his greatest success as an Indian nationalist. He persuaded even those Muslim representatives at the Conference, who had long been opponents of joint electorates, to agree to them, provided the Hindu leaders reciprocated, by agreeing to certain minority safeguards for the Muslims. . . . Gandhi adopted a *non-possumus* attitude and preferred to return home empty-handed rather than settle with the Muslims. From now on the policy of Gandhi and the Congress Party was to try to appease the Muslims, not by settling with them, but by taking them from hope to hope and promise to promise.

Gandhi and the Congress: A Hindu Nationalist View

V. D. SAVARKAR

The preceding selection reflected Gandhi's failure to satisfy Muslim opinion. Yet it is interesting to note that Gandhi also faced criticism from the other side as well. Some Hindus were disturbed by his unorthodox outlook on social and religious matters, such as Untouchability, while others attacked his approaches to Indian Muslims as a betrayal of the legitimate interests of the Hindu majority. The latter viewpoint is suggested by the following excerpt from V. D. Savarkar's presidential address to the Hindu *Mahasabha* in 1939, in which he criticized Gandhi's support of the *Khilafat* movement in the early 1920's. Savarkar (1883–   ), a pioneer figure of militant nationalism, had been imprisoned for anti-British activities from 1911 to 1924, and on his release he was debarred from political activity until 1937. When the restriction was lifted, he was immediately chosen as the leader of the *Mahasabha*, an organization which championed an avowedly Hindu nationalism.

I HAVE no space here nor the inclination to frame a charge-sheet against the Congress, enumerating the grievous errors it has been committing under the dictatorship of Gandhiji and the leaders of his persuasion ever since the *Khilafat* agitation. . . . It is not their motive but their judgment and in a couple of cases a monomaniac incompetence which were responsible for the erroneous policy they persisted in which has done incalculable harm to the Hindu cause and which if not checkmated is likely to jeopardize not only the legitimate interests of Hindudom far more dangerously than in the past but even the vital interests of the "Indian Nation" too as the Congress itself understands it and loves so well.

It is not, therefore, to rake up fruitlessly the sad memories of the most grievous errors which the Congressites committed in their identification with the *Khilafat* agitation but to warn against the imminent dangers of a similar type that I must refer to a few facts regarding the attitude of the Gandhist politicians in that ill-fated movement. In spite of the warnings of the Great Tilak, Gandhiji committed the Congress to the purely communal, religious and extraterritorial *Khilafat* agitation to placate the Muslims and himself went to the length of insisting on the point that the question of *swaraj* itself should be subordinated to the *Khilafat* issue — nay, he said it was the religious duty of the Hindus to help the *Khalipha!* . . . These Congressite Hindu leaders did not subordinate *swaraj* to the *Khilafat* question only in its figurative aspect but were hand in glove with the Muslim leaders who instigated Amir Ama-

From V. D. Savarkar, *Hindu Rashtra Darshan* (Bombay, 1949), pp. 124–129. By permission of Laxman Ganesh Khare.

nullakhan [of Afghanistan] to invade India as he actually did. We have the word of Swami Shradhanandji for it. The Swamiji publicly wrote to that effect in protest in his *Liberator* and produced some documentary evidence and a draft telegram in Gandhiji's handwriting to the Amir which Maulana Mahomad Ali had shown to Swamiji. In his own *Young India* Gandhiji admitted that the Afghans if successful were sure to establish their Kingdom in India — and yet these Congressite Hindu leaders did not dissociate themselves from the Muslim leaders in their open and secret activities to egg on the Afghan Invasion, but on the contrary promised support to this treacherous move. Gandhiji writes in his *Young India*

I would in a sense certainly assist the Amir of Afghanistan if he waged war against the British government — by openly telling my countrymen that it would be a crime to help the government, etc. . . .

What is most surprising to note is the fact that these Hindu leaders outbid even the Ali Brothers, the "National" Maulana Azad and other Muslim leaders in maintaining that if the Amir succeeded in capturing Delhi, we would have won *swaraj* — for, they definitely stated that the rule of the Afghans was in itself a *swaraj* — "We Hindu Muslims are one — an indivisible Nation." I vividly remember conversations I had with these Hindu leaders of Gandhist persuasion when they used to meet me then in prison. How expectantly they waited for the invading armies of the Amir to capture Lahore! Well, after all the *Khilaphat* was guillotined by the Turks themselves and the Amir Amanullah instead of being an Emperor at Delhi was dethroned by a Baccha Saku in Kabul itself; and all that India reaped from the *Khilaphat* agitation was the intensified Pan-Islamic fanaticism roused by that movement amongst the Indian Muslims all over India, aided and abetted by the Hindus themselves who paid dearly for this their

folly there and then in Malabar, Kohat, Punjab, Bengal — and will have yet to pay unless they learn to react.

While the *Khilaphat* was on his brain, in a reply he gave to the correspondent of the *Daily Express,* London, Gandhiji disclosed his plan of converting the Afghans from fanatical turbulence into a peaceful citizenship thus,

I would introduce the spinning wheel amongst the Afghan tribes also and then that will prevent them from attacking Indian territory. I feel the tribesmen are in their own way God-fearing people.

Yes, "in their own way": That is the trouble. For, we can clearly discern their own way of God-fearingness in the ghastly light of Hindu habitations set on fire throughout the frontier line from Sindh to Kashmere. Only Hindus looted, only Hindus killed, only Hindu women and men kidnaped!! Is not the Fakir of Ipi also a God-fearing man in his own way? And the spinning wheel to persuade them from attacking India! How many centuries after, Sir? And what are we Hindus to do in the meanwhile? To garrison the frontiers with hosts of Hindu damsels with the charm of the spinning wheel in their hands — as Gandhiji has suggested quite seriously at one of the sittings of the Round Table Conference?

Well, gentlemen, I am not referring to these few details in any light mood. I want you to realise the mentality and the ideology of these Hindu leaders who happen to be at the helm of the Congress. Neither Gandhiji or Pandit Nehru, nay, not even Subhas Babu or Mr. Roy who, although they do not contribute in any way to some of the above vagaries of the Gandhist school, are still votaries — I call it victims — of the school of thought which says in so many words, "Give to the Moslems so much that they could not wish to ask for anything more." They may sincerely believe that to be the crux of nationalism and wisdom. But do you, who do not wish to see Hindudom humiliated and browbeaten into servility, believe it to be so? If not, are you going to authorise these very gentlemen by electing and returning them as representatives who can speak in the name of the Hindus once again at any Round Table Conference to come, to enter into any new pact with the Moslems on behalf of the Hindus or entrust the destiny of the Northwestern Frontiers into the hands of the Khan brothers who are the Congress Plenipotentiaries and Gandhiji's certified lieutenants there — as once the Ali Brothers were? I call upon those thousands of Hindus also who have not ceased to be Hindus but who still follow the Congress with a blind habitual trait to ponder as seriously as possible on these questions.

What Congress and Gandhi Have Done to the Untouchables

B. R. AMBEDKAR

No aspect of Gandhi's activities for social reform has been so widely acclaimed as his efforts on behalf of the Untouchables. It is ironic, therefore, that one of his most bitter critics should have been a man who was himself an Untouchable, B. R. Ambedkar (1893–1956), the leader of the All-India Depressed Classes Federation. Ambedkar, the holder of earned doctorates from both Columbia University and the University of London, climaxed his career by serving as Chairman of the Drafting Committee of India's Constituent Assembly and holding office as Minister of Law in Nehru's cabinet from 1947 to 1951. The expression of his views presented here is taken from his book, *What Congress and Gandhi Have Done to the Untouchables* (1945).

M R. Gandhi's views on the caste system — which constitutes the main social problem in India — were fully elaborated by him in 1921–22 in a Gujarati journal called *Nava-Jivan*. The article is written in Gujarati. I give below an English translation of his views as near as possible in his own words. Says Mr. Gandhi:

(1) I believe that if Hindu Society has been able to stand it is because it is founded on the caste system.

(2) The seeds of *swaraj* are to be found in the caste system. Different castes are like different sections of military division. Each division is working for the good of the whole. . . .

(3) A community which can create the caste system must be said to possess unique power of organization.

(4) Caste has a ready made means for spreading primary education. Every caste can take the responsibility for the education of the children of the caste. Caste has a political basis. It can work as an electorate for a representative body. Caste can perform judicial functions by electing persons to act as judges to decide disputes among members of the

From B. R. Ambedkar, *What Congress and Gandhi Have Done to the Untouchables,* 2nd edition (Bombay, 1946), pp. 286–290, 293–297, 300–308. Reprinted by permission of Thacker & Co., Ltd., Bombay.

same caste. With castes it is easy to raise a defense force by requiring each caste to raise a brigade.

(5) I believe that interdining or intermarriage are not necessary for promoting national unity. That dining together creates friendship is contrary to experience. If this was true there would have been no war in Europe. . . . Taking food is as dirty an act as answering the call of nature. The only difference is that after answering call of nature we get peace while after eating food we get discomfort. Just as we perform the act of answering the call of nature in seclusion so also the act of taking food must also be done in seclusion.

(6) In India children of brothers do not intermarry. Do they cease to love because they do not intermarry? Among the *Vaishnavas* many women are so orthodox that they will not eat with members of the family nor will they drink water from a common water pot. Have they no love? The caste system cannot be said to be bad because it does not allow interdining or intermarriage between different castes.

(7) Caste is another name for control. Caste puts a limit on enjoyment. Caste does not allow a person to transgress caste limits in pursuit of his enjoyment. That is the meaning of such caste restrictions as interdining and intermarriage.

(8) To destroy caste system and adopt Western European social system means that Hindus must give up the principle of hereditary occupation which is the soul of the caste system. Hereditary principle is an eternal principle. To change it is to create disorder. I have no use for a *Brahmin* if I cannot call him a *Brahmin* for my life. It will be a chaos if every day a *Brahmin* is to be changed into a *Shudra* and a *Shudra* is to be changed into a *Brahmin*.

(9) The caste system is a natural order of society. In India it has been given a religious coating. Other countries not having understood the utility of the caste system, it existed only in a loose condition and consequently those countries have not derived from caste system the same degree of advantage which India has derived.

These being my views I am opposed to all those who are out to destroy the caste system.

In 1922, Mr. Gandhi was a defender of the caste system. Pursuing the inquiry, one comes across a somewhat critical view of the caste system by Mr. Gandhi in the year 1925. This is what Mr. Gandhi said on 3rd February 1925:

I gave support to caste because it stands for restraint. But at present caste does not mean restraint, it means limitations. Restraint is glorious and helps to achieve freedom. But limitation is like chain. It binds. There is nothing commendable in castes as they exist to-day. They are contrary to the tenets of the *Shastras*. The number of castes is infinite and there is a bar against intermarriage. This is not a condition of elevation. It is a state of fall.

In reply to the question: What is the way out? Mr. Gandhi said:

The best remedy is that small castes should fuse themselves into one big caste. There should be four such big castes so that we may reproduce the old system of four *Varnas*.

In short, in 1925 Mr. Gandhi became an upholder of the *Varna* system.

The old *Varna* system prevalent in ancient India had the society divided into four orders: (1) *Brahmins,* whose occupation was learning; (2) *Kshatriyas,* whose occupation was warfare; (3) *Vaishyas,* whose occupation was trade and (4) *Shudras,* whose occupation was service of the other classes. Is Mr. Gandhi's *Varna* system the same as this old *Varna* system of the orthodox Hindus? Mr. Gandhi explained his *Varna* system in the following terms:

(1) I believe that the divisions into *Varna* is based on birth.

(2) There is nothing in the *Varna* system which stands in the way of the *Shudra* acquiring learning or studying military art of offense or defense. Contra it is open to a *Kshatriya* to serve. The *Varna* system is no bar to him. What the *Varna* system enjoins is that a *Shudra* will not make learning a way of earning a living. Nor will a *Kshatriya* adopt

service as a way of earning a living. [Similarly a *Brahmin* may learn the art of war or trade. But he must not make them a way of earning his living. Contra a *Va·shya* may acquire learning or may cultivate the art of war. But he must not make them a way of earning his living.]

(3) The *Varna* system is connected with the way of earning a living. There is no harm if a person belonging to one *Varna* acquires the knowledge or science and art specialized in by persons belonging to other *Varnas*. But as far as the way of earning his living is concerned he must follow the occupation of the *Varna* to which he belongs which means he must follow the hereditary profession of his forefathers.

(4) The object of the *Varna* system is to prevent competition and class struggle and class war. I believe in the *Varna* system because it fixes the duties and occupations of persons.

(5) *Varna* means the determination of a man's occupation before he is born.

(6) In the *Varna* system no man has any liberty to choose his occupation. His occupation is determined for him by heredity.

*   *   *

The social ideal of Gandhism is either caste or *Varna*. Though it may be difficult to say which, there can be no doubt that the social ideal of Gandhism is not democracy. For, whether one takes for comparison caste or *Varna* both are fundamentally opposed to democracy. . . .

That Mr. Gandhi changed over from the caste system to the *Varna* system does not make the slightest difference to the charge that Gandhism is opposed to democracy. In the first place, the idea of *Varna* is the parent of the idea of caste. If the idea of caste is a pernicious idea it is entirely because of the viciousness of the idea of *Varna*. Both are evil ideas and it matters very little whether one believes in *Varna* or in caste.

*   *   *

Turning to the field of economic life, Mr. Gandhi stands for two ideals. One of these is the opposition to machinery . . . evidenced by his idolization of *charkha* (the spinning wheel) and by insistence upon hand-spinning and hand-weaving. His opposition to machinery and his love for *charkha* are not a matter of accident. They are a matter of his philosophy of life. . . .

The second ideal of Mr. Gandhi is the elimination of class war and even class struggle in the relationship between employers and employees and between landlords and tenants. . . . Mr. Gandhi does not wish to hurt the propertied class. He is even opposed to a campaign against them. He has no passion for economic equality. Referring to the propertied class Mr. Gandhi said quite recently that he does not wish to destroy the hen that lays the golden egg. His solution for the economic conflict between the owners and the workers, between the rich and the poor, between the landlords and the tenants and between the employers and the employees is very simple. The owners need not deprive themselves of their property. All that they need do is to declare themselves trustees for the poor. Of course, the trust is to be a voluntary one carrying only a spiritual obligation.

Is there anything new in the Gandhian analysis of economic ills? Are the economics of Gandhism sound? What hope does Gandhism hold out to the common man, to the down and out? Does it promise him a better life, a life of joy and culture, a life of freedom, not merely freedom from want but freedom to rise, to grow to the full stature which his capacities can reach?

There is nothing new in the Gandhian analysis of economic ills, insofar as it attributes them to machinery and the civilization that is built upon it. That machinery and modern civilization help to concentrate management and control into relatively few hands, and with the aid of banking and credit facilitate the transfer into still fewer hands of all materials and factories and mills in which millions are bled white in order to support huge industries thousands of miles away from their cottages, maimings and cripplings far in excess of the corresponding injuries by war, and are responsible for disease and physical deterioration due directly and indirectly to the development of large cities with their smoke, dirt, noise, foul air, lack of sunshine and outdoor life, slums, prostitution and unnatural living which they bring about, are all old and worn-out arguments. There is nothing new in them. Gandhism is merely repeating the views of Rousseau, Ruskin, Tolstoy and their school.

The ideas which go to make up Gandhism are just primitive. It is a return to nature, to animal life. Their only merit is their simplicity. As there is always a large corps of simple people who are attracted by them, such simple ideas do not die, and there is always some simpleton to preach them. There is, however, no doubt that the practical instincts of men — which seldom go wrong — have found them unfruitful and which society in search of progress has thought it best to reject.

The economics of Gandhism are hopelessly fallacious. The fact that machinery and modern civilization have produced many evils may be admitted. But these evils are no argument against them. For the evils are not due to machinery and modern civilization. They are due to wrong social organization, which has made private property and pursuit of personal gain, matters of absolute sanctity. If machinery and civilization have not benefited everybody, the remedy is not to condemn machinery and civilization but to alter the organization of society so that the benefits will not be usurped by the few but will accrue to all.

In Gandhism, the common man has no hope. It treats man as an animal and no more. It is true that man shares the constitution and functions of animals, nutritive, reproductive, etc. But these are not distinctively human functions. The distinctively human function is reason, the purpose of which is to enable man to observe, meditate, cogitate, study and discover the beauties of the Universe and enrich his life and control the animal elements in his life. Man thus occupies the highest place in the scheme of animate existence. If this is true what is the conclusion that follows: The conclusion that follows is that while the ultimate goal of a brute's life is reached once his physical appetites are satisfied, the ultimate goal of man's existence is not reached unless and until he has fully cultivated his mind. In short, what divides the brute from man is culture. Culture is not possible for the brute, but it is essential for man. That being so, the aim of human society must be to enable every person to lead a life of culture, which means the cultivation of mind as distinguished from the satisfaction of mere physical wants. How can this happen?

Both for society as well as for individual[s] there is always a gulf between merely living and living worthily. In order that one may live worthily one must first live. The time and energy spent upon mere life, upon gaining of subsistence detracts from that available for activities of a distinctively human nature and which go to make up a life of culture. How then can a life of culture be made possible? It is not possible unless there is sufficient leisure. For, it is only when there is leisure that a person is free to devote himself to a life of culture. The problem of all problems, which human society has to face, is how to provide leisure to every individual. What does leisure mean? Leisure means the lessening of the toil and effort necessary for satisfying the physical wants of life. How can leisure be made possible? Leisure is quite impossible unless some means are found whereby the toil required for producing goods necessary to satisfy human needs is lessened. What can lessen such toil? Only when machine takes the place of man. There is no other means of producing leisure. Machinery and modern civilization are thus indispensable for emancipating man from leading the life of a brute, and for providing him with leisure and for making a life of culture possible. The man who condemns machinery and modern civilization simply does not understand their purpose and the ultimate aim which human society must strive to achieve.

Gandhism may be well suited to a society which does not accept democracy as its ideal. A society which does not believe in democracy may be indifferent to machinery and the civilization based upon it. But a democratic society cannot. The former may well content itself with a life of leisure and culture for the few and a life of toil and drudgery for the many. But a democratic society must assure a life of leisure and culture to each one of its citizens. If the above analysis is correct then the slogan of a democratic society must be machinery, and more machinery, civilization and more civilization. Under Gandhism the common man must keep on toiling ceaselessly for a pittance and remain a brute. In short, Gandhism with its call of back to nature, means back to nakedness, back to squalor, back to poverty and back to ignorance for the vast mass of the people. . . .

Gandhism insists upon class structure. It regards the class structure of society and also the income structure as sacrosanct with the consequent distinctions of rich and poor, high and low, owners and workers, as permanent parts of social organization. From the point of view of social consequences, nothing can be more pernicious. . . . It is not enough to say that Gandhism believes in a class structure. Gandhism stands for more than that. A class structure which is a faded, jejune, effete thing — a mere sentimentality, a mere skeleton is not what Gandhism wants. It wants class structure to function as a living faith. In this there is nothing to be surprised at. For, class structure in Gandhism is not a mere accident. It is its official doctrine.

The idea of trusteeship, which Gandhism proposes as a panacea and by which the moneyed classes will hold their properties in trust for the poor, is the most ridiculous part of it. All that one can say

about it is that if anybody else had propounded it the author would have been laughed at as a silly fool, who had not known the hard realities of life and was deceiving the servile classes by telling them that a little dose of moral rearmament to the propertied classes — those who by their insatiable cupidity and indomitable arrogance have made and will always make this world a vale of tears for the toiling millions — will recondition them to such an extent that they will be able to withstand the temptation to misuse the tremendous powers which the class structure gives them over servile classes. . . .

Mr. Gandhi sometimes speaks on social and economic subjects as though he was a blushing Red. Those who will study Gandhism will not be deceived by the occasional aberrations of Mr. Gandhi in favour of democracy and against capitalism. For, Gandhism is in no sense a revolutionary creed. It is conservatism *in excelsis*. So far as India is concerned, it is a reactionary creed blazoning on its banner the call of Return to Antiquity. Gandhism aims at the resuscitation and reanimation of India's dread, dying past.

Gandhism is a paradox. It stands for freedom from foreign domination, which means the destruction of the existing political structure of the country. At the same time, it seeks to maintain intact a social structure which permits the domination of one class by another on a hereditary basis which means a perpetual domination of one class by another. . . .

The first special feature of Gandhism is that its philosophy helps those who want to keep what they have and to prevent those who have not from getting what they have a right to get. No one who examines the Gandhian attitude to strikes, the Gandhian reverence for caste and the Gandhian doctrine of Trusteeship by the rich for the benefit of the poor can deny that this is an upshot of Gandhism. Whether this is the calculated result of a deliberate design or whether it is a matter of accident may be open to argument. But the fact remains that Gandhism is the philosophy of the well-to-do and the leisure class.

The second special feature of Gandhism is to delude people into accepting their misfortunes by presenting them as best of good fortunes. One or two illustrations will suffice to bring out the truth of this statement.

The Hindu sacred law penalized the Shudras (Hindus of the fourth class) from acquiring wealth. It is a law of enforced poverty unknown in any other part of the world. What does Gandhism do? It does not lift the ban. It blesses the Shudra for his moral courage to give up property. It is well worth quoting Mr. Gandhi's own words. Here they are:

The Shudra who only serves (the higher caste) as a matter of religious duty, and who will never own any property, who indeed has not even the ambition to own anything, is deserving of thousand obeisances. . . . The very Gods will shower down flowers on him.

Another illustration in support is the attitude of Gandhism towards the scavenger. The sacred law of the Hindus lays down that a scavenger's progeny shall live by scavenging. Under Hinduism scavenging was not a matter of choice, it was a matter of force. What does Gandhism do? It seeks to perpetuate this system by praising scavenging as the noblest service to society! Let me quote Mr. Gandhi: As a President of a Conference of the Untouchables, Mr. Gandhi said:

I do not want to attain Moksha. I do not want to be reborn. But if I have to be reborn, I should be born an untouchable, so that I may share their sorrows, sufferings and the affronts levelled at them, in order that I may endeavor to free myself and them from that miserable condition. I, therefore prayed that if I should be born again, I should do so not as a Brahmin, Kshatriya, Vaishya, or Shudra, but as an Atishudra. . . .

I love scavenging. In my ashram, an eighteen-years-old Brahmin lad is doing the scavenger's work in order to teach the ashram scavenger cleanliness. The lad is no reformer. He was born and bred in orthodoxy. . . . But he felt that his accomplishments were incomplete until he had become also a perfect sweeper, and that, if he wanted the ashram sweeper to do his work well, he must do it himself and set an example.

You should realize that you are cleaning Hindu Society.

Can there be a worse example of false propaganda than this attempt of Gandhism to perpetuate evils which have been deliberately imposed by one class over another? If Gandhism preached the rule of poverty for all and not merely for the Shudra the worst that could be said about it is that it is a mistaken idea. But why preach it as good for one class only? . . . In India a man is not a scavenger because of his work. He is a scavenger because of his birth irrespective of the question whether he does scavenging or not. If Gandhism preached that scavenging is a noble profession with the object of inducing those who refuse to engage in it, one could understand it. But why appeal to the scavenger's pride and vanity in order to induce him and him only to keep on to scavenging by telling him that scavenging is a noble profession and that he need not be ashamed of it? To preach that poverty is good for the Shudra and for none else, to preach that scavenging is good for the Untouchables and for none else and to make them accept these onerous impositions as voluntary purposes of life, by appeal to their failings is an outrage and a cruel joke on the helpless classes which none but Mr. Gandhi can perpetrate with equanimity and impunity. . . .

Criticism apart, this is the technique of Gandhism, to make wrongs done appear to the very victim as though they were his privileges. If there is an "ism" which has made full use of religion as an opium to lull the people into false beliefs and false security, it is Gandhism. Following Shakespeare, one can well say: Plausibility! Ingenuity! Thy name is Gandhism.

Such is Gandhism. Having known what is Gandhism the answer to the question, "Should Gandhism become the law of the land what would be the lot of the Untouchables under it?" cannot require much scratching of the brain. . . . In India even the lowest man among the caste Hindus — why even the aboriginal and the Hill Tribe man — though educationally and economically not very much above the Untouchables is still superior to the Untouchables. The Hindu society accepts his claim to superiority over the Untouchables. The Untouchable will therefore continue to suffer the worst fate as he does now namely, in prosperity he will be the last to be employed and in depression the first to be fired.

What does Gandhism do to relieve the Untouchables from this fate? Gandhism professes to abolish Untouchability. That is hailed as the greatest virtue of Gandhism. But what does this virtue amount to in actual life? To assess the value of this anti-Untouchability which is regarded as a very big element in Gandhism, it is necessary to understand fully the scope of Mr. Gandhi's programme for the removal of Untouchability. Does it mean anything more than that the Hindus will not mind touching the Untouchables? Does it mean the removal of the ban on the right of the Untouchables to education? It would be better to take the two questions separately.

To start with the first question. Mr. Gandhi does not say that a Hindu should not take a bath after touching the Untouchables. If Mr. Gandhi does not object to it as a purification of pollution then it is difficult to see how Untouchability can be said to vanish by touching the Untouchables. Untouchability centers round the idea of pollution by contact and purification by bath to remove the pollution. Does it mean social assimilation of the Untouchables with the Hindus? Mr. Gandhi has most categorically stated that removal of Untouchability does not mean interdining or intermarriage between the Hindus and the Untouchables. Mr. Gandhi's anti-Untouchability means that the Untouchables will be classed as *Shudras* instead of being classed as *Atishudras* [i.e., "beyond *Shudras*"]. There is nothing more in it. Mr. Gandhi has not considered whether the old *Shudras* will accept the new *Shudras* into their fold. If they don't then the removal of Untouchability is a senseless proposition for it will still keep the Untouchables as a separate social category. Mr. Gandhi probably knows that the abolition of Untouchability will not bring about the assimilation of the Untouchables by the *Shudras*. That seems to be the reason why Mr. Gandhi himself has given a new and a different name to the Untouchables. The new name registers by anticipation what is likely to be the fact. By calling the Untouchables *Harijans,* Mr. Gandhi has killed two birds with one stone. He has shown that assimilation of the Untouchables by the *Shudras* is not possible. He has also by his new name counteracted assimilation and made it impossible.

Regarding the second question, it is true that Gandhism is prepared to remove the old ban placed by the Hindu *Shastras* on the right of the Untouchables to education and permit them to acquire knowledge and learning. Under Gandhism the Untouchables may study law, they may study medicine, they may study engineering or anything else they may fancy. So far so good. But will the Untouchables be free to make use of their knowledge and learning? Will they have the right to choose their profession? Can they adopt the career of lawyer, doctor or engineer? To these questions the answer which Gandhism gives is an emphatic "no." The Untouchables must follow their hereditary professions. That those occupations are unclean is no excuse. That before the occupation became hereditary it was the result of force and not volition does not matter. The argument of Gandhism is that what is once settled is settled forever even if it was wrongly settled. Under Gandhism the Untouchables are to be eternal scavengers. There is no doubt that the Untouchables would much prefer the orthodox system of Untouchability. A compulsory state of ignorance imposed upon the Untouchables by the Hindu *Shastras* made scavenging bearable. But Gandhism which compels an educated Untouchable to do scavenging is nothing short of cruelty. The grace in Gandhism is a curse in its worst form. The virtue of the anti-Untouchability plank in Gandhism is quite illusory. There is no substance in it.

What else is there in Gandhism which the Untouchables can accept as opening a way for their ultimate salvation? Barring this illusory campaign against Untouchability, Gandhism is simply another form of Sanatanism which is the ancient name for militant orthodox Hinduism. What is there in Gandhism which is not to be found in orthodox Hinduism? There is caste in Hinduism, there is caste in Gandhism. Hinduism believes in the law of hereditary profession, so does Gandhism. Hinduism enjoins cow-worship. So does Gandhism. Hinduism upholds the law of *karma*, predestination of man's condition in this world, so does Gandhism. Hinduism accepts the authority of the *Shastras*. So does Gandhism. Hinduism believes in idols. So does Gandhism. All that Gandhism has done is to find a philosophic justification for Hinduism and its dogmas. Hinduism is bald in the sense that it is just a set of rules which bear on their face the appearance of a crude and cruel system. Gandhism supplies the philosophy which smoothens its surface and gives it the appearance of decency and respectability and so alters it and embellishes it as to make it even attractive. . . .

What hope can Gandhism offer to the Untouchables? To the Untouchables, Hinduism is a veritable chamber of horrors. The sanctity and infallibility of the Vedas, Smritis and Shastras, the iron law of caste, the heartless law of *karma* and the senseless law of status by birth are to the Untouchables veritable instruments of torture which Hinduism has forged against the Untouchables. These very instruments which have mutilated, blasted and blighted the life of the Untouchables are to be found intact and untarnished in the bosom of Gandhism. How can the Untouchables say that Gandhism is a heaven and not a chamber of horrors as Hinduism has been? The only reaction and a very natural reaction of the Untouchables would be to run away from Gandhism.

Gandhists may say that what I have stated applies to the old type of Gandhism. There is a new Gandhism, Gandhism without caste. This has reference to the recent statement of Mr. Gandhi that caste is an anachronism. Reformers were naturally gladdened by this declaration of Mr. Gandhi. And who would not be glad to see that a man like Mr. Gandhi having such terrible influence over the Hindus, after having played the most mischievous part of a social reactionary, after having stood out as the protagonist of the caste system, after having beguiled and befooled the unthinking Hindus with arguments which made no distinction between what is fair and foul should have come out with this recantation? But is this really a matter for jubilation? Does it change the nature of Gandhism? Does it make Gandhism a new and a better "ism" than it was before? Those who are carried away by this recantation of Mr. Gandhi, forget two things. In the first place, all that Mr. Gandhi has said is that caste is an anachronism. He does not say it is an evil. He does not say it is anathema. Mr. Gandhi may be taken to be not in favour of caste. But Mr. Gandhi does not say that he is against the *Varna* system. And what is Mr. Gandhi's *Varna* system? It is simply a new name for the caste system and retains all the worst features of the caste system.

The declaration of Mr. Gandhi cannot be taken to mean any fundamental change in Gandhism. It cannot make Gandhism acceptable to the Untouchables. The Untouchables will still have ground to say: "Good God! Is this man Gandhi our Saviour?"

REASSESSMENTS IN RETROSPECT

Gandhi's Place in the History of Indian Nationalism

R. C. MAJUMDAR

The first group of readings in this volume presented the views of Gandhi's supporters and followers; the second, the arguments of his critics. While some of the selections in these first two sections were written after Gandhi's assassination, they all reflect attitudes which were current during his lifetime. As the Gandhian era recedes into the past, new perspectives become possible on Gandhi's role in the development of modern India. The readings in this third section illustrate a variety of recent interpretations.

The opening selection is from R. C. Majumdar (1888–), one of India's most distinguished historians who is widely known and respected for his studies of ancient India. In his later years, Dr. Majumdar has turned his attention to the history of Indian nationalism, raising challenging questions which are bound to provoke continuing controversy. The selection which follows is drawn from two sources, the preface to Volume III of his *History of the Freedom Movement in India* (1963) and the concluding section of *Three Phases of India's Struggle for Freedom* (1961).

GANDHI combined in himself the dual role of a saint and an active politician. He has been called by some "the most saintly among politicians," and by others, "the most political saint." This shows the paradoxical nature of his personality. Whether such combination is good or bad need not be discussed here, but it poses a serious problem to the historian. One's attitude towards a saint or view of his personal conduct and career is a matter of devotion and personal opinion. But one's judgment on the public career of a political leader rests upon certain assumptions and expectations of a norm of conduct to be followed by him. The former is based upon faith, pure and simple, while the latter requires logical reasoning untrammelled by any personal sentiment or belief. The historian has nothing to do with the first, and is concerned only with the second aspect. Unfortunately, Gandhi's followers did not make this distinction and gave unto the political leader what was really due to the saint. . . . A mystic or saint — such as Gandhi undoubtedly was — is beyond the purview of political history, but in dealing with Gandhi as the great leader of the Indian National Congress, a purely political organization fighting for freedom from British yoke, history must apply to him the same standards of judgment and criticism as have been applied to all other personalities, great or small, who have played any role in political affairs. Sober history must subject the public life of Gandhi to a critical and rational review without passion or prejudice, uninfluenced in the least by personal feelings of admiration or devotion, and, above all, by

From R. C. Majumdar, *History of the Freedom Movement in India*, Volume III (Calcutta, 1963), pp. xv–xxv, xxix–xxxi, and R. C. Majumdar, *Three Phases of India's Struggle for Freedom* (Bombay, 1961), pp. 40–44, 47–61. By permission of the author and of Bharatiya Vidya Bhavan, Bombay.

a disposition or proneness to believe as right and proper whatever he might have chosen to do or say. Such history must begin by discounting the halo of semi-divinity — and therefore also of infallibility — which was cast round Gandhi during his life and continues to a large extent even now, thanks to the propaganda to exploit his name for political purposes.

I yield to none in my profound respect for Gandhi, the saint and the humanitarian. But as the author of this volume, I am only concerned with the part he played in the struggle for India's freedom from the British yoke. I have necessarily to view his life and activities, thoughts, and feelings primarily from a narrow angle, namely as a politician and statesman leading a great political organization which was not intended to be a humanitarian association or World Peace Society, but had been formed for a definite political object, namely, to achieve India's freedom from political bondage. It has been my painful duty to show that, looked at strictly from this point of view, the popular image of Gandhi cannot be reconciled with what he actually was. A historian must uphold the great ideal of truth which was so dear to Gandhi himself, and if we delineate the political life of Gandhi with strict adherence to truth, the whole truth and nothing but the truth, it will, I believe, be patent to all that Gandhi was lacking in both political wisdom and political strategy — as we commonly understand these terms — and far from being infallible, committed serious blunders, one after another, in pursuit of some Utopian ideals and methods which had no basis in reality. It will also be seen that the current estimate of the degree or extent of his success bears no relation to actual facts.

I am not unaware of the rude shock that such treatment would give to a large section of Indians and the great probability that they would curse or at least denounce the author without perhaps even going through the book itself. But I am sustained by two considerations. In the first place, I

have sincerely tried to uphold the dignity of history by telling the truth as it has appeared to me in the light of such judgment or intellect as God has vouchsafed to me. I have done no less — I could do no more. Secondly, the adverse criticisms I have made against Gandhi — and the most serious ones at that — have almost all been upheld by one or more of his most admiring devotees, perhaps in some unguarded moments of their lives or when they were free from the magic influence of their political *Guru*. It has been my endeavour to keep this fact constantly before the readers by extensive quotations, so that I may not be accused of any deliberate ill-will or malice against Gandhi. I have thus quoted, in support of my criticisms, those of even such devotees as Pandit Motilal Nehru, Jawaharlal Nehru, C. R. Das, Rajagopalachari, and Sardar Vallabhbhai Patel, among others, not to speak of hostile critics like Subhas Bose, Sir Sankaran Nair, K. F. Nariman, and Ambedkar. The adverse criticisms by the devotees were, of course, merely occasional lapses which did not affect in the least their unflinching faith in the leadership of Gandhi. Nevertheless, the quotations of their views would prove that I cannot — and I certainly do not — claim any credit and do not deserve discredit for originality in the views condemning Gandhi, however unpalatable they might appear when taken together in the mass.

In order to enable the reader to appreciate or assess properly the views on Gandhi expressed in this volume, I would like to explain here my general estimate of Gandhi as a political leader which is naturally obscured in the text by the narration of events in a chronological order.

Since 1919 the Indian National Congress, under the leadership of Gandhi, had developed into a fighting machine and revolutionary organization, nonviolent in character but of tremendous strength and potentiality, on account of the mass support behind it. The ground for the popular upsurge was prepared beforehand as described in the preceding volume, but Gandhi's magic personality and saintly character, which has always a great appeal to Indian masses, transformed the latent energy of the people into strenuous political activity in an astonishingly short period of time. The two new weapons with which Gandhi decided to fight were nonviolent, non-co-operation and civil disobedience — the two outward manifestations of the great principle which Gandhi described as *satyagraha*. It was an old principle which, according to Gandhi, was preached by the Indian sages of yore, but he was the first to use it in politics. . . . It would be obvious to anybody who understands its real significance that none but a saintly person can really observe it in actual life, and it was beyond the power of ordinary men, including even those who played a prominent role in Indian politics under Gandhi's leadership. They made no secret of the fact that they adopted nonviolent non-cooperation as a political expedient but not, like Gandhi, as a creed. Gandhi himself admitted, even late in life, that none of his followers believed in *satyagraha* as a creed, though some accepted it as a political expediency in the absence of any more suitable way to fight the battle of India's freedom — implying thereby that they would change it the moment they felt that some other course of action would be more helpful in achieving freedom. This was the reason why, as Gandhi himself admitted, "even 14 years of trial have failed to yield the anticipated result."

There is a popular notion, sustained by catching slogans, that Gandhi achieved India's freedom by the method of *satyagraha* and thus laid down for the subject peoples all over the world a unique method for gaining independence without bloodshed. Of course, Gandhi's own statement leaves no doubt that *satyagraha* had never any fair trial in India's struggle for freedom, and, as such, cannot claim any credit for it.

But there were other deep-seated differences between Gandhi and his followers. He placed the cult of nonviolence above everything else — even above the inde-

pendence of India. During the Second War he grew uneasy at the possibility that the British might grant independence to India, for that would mean India's participation in violent warfare. To him the Congress was a humanitarian association or an organization for the moral and spiritual regeneration of the world, and its aims and activities were to be regulated accordingly. But his followers looked upon the Congress as a purely political body whose sole object — and *raison d'être* — was the achievement of the freedom of India. . . . As a matter of fact Gandhi realised, late in life, that a wide gulf had always separated him from his followers though they all submitted to his authority. . . . This fact would have been apparent to Gandhi long before if the Congress were guided by him on democratic principles. But Gandhi was a dictator who could not tolerate opposition. In 1930 he deliberately excluded from the Working Committee of the Congress those who differed from his views. In his lengthy statement issued on 17 September, 1934, Gandhi said that if the Socialist Group gained ascendancy in the Congress he could not remain in it. Later, when one of his momentous decisions was opposed by Azad and Nehru he demanded that both should leave the Working Committee, and even formally wrote to Azad asking him to resign the Presidentship of the Congress. The scene[1] that he created after the meeting of the A.I.C.C. [All-India Congress Committee] at Ahmadabad on 27 June, 1924 hardly befits a democratic leader. It is difficult to improve upon the following words with which Pyarelal, a close associate of Gandhi, has described the resulting state of things:

Gandhiji came to the conclusion that his personality was acting as an incubus and

---

[1] The reference is to Gandhi's emotional disturbance when 70 out of 148 members of the Committee voted in favor of a resolution which would have expressed qualified approval of the politically-motivated murder of an Englishman by Gopinath Saha. [Editor's note]

smothering free self-expression in the Congress and thereby arresting its natural growth, so that from being "the most representative and democratic organisation" it stood in danger of degenerating into an organisation "dominated by one personality" in which "there was no play of reason." They could never realise the full potency of truth or non-violence that way. For that they had "to think and act naturally."

This fully supports what has been said above of blind faith in Gandhi. One of his admiring devotees referred to him as "beloved slave-driver." Gandhi realized at long last that slave-driving may be an agreeable pastime and a great source of strength to a leader, but it does not pay in the long run. For, like ordinary slaves, the slave-followers of Gandhi gradually turned against his leadership and revolted against his authority.

It is not often realized by many that since the failure of the "Quit India" movement Gandhi's political influence waned more and more as the achievement of freedom approached nearer and nearer. He had very little share in the Congress negotiations with Cripps and practically none in those vital and momentous decisions which finally led to the freedom of India.

*   *   *

The two great ends of Gandhi's life, to which even the freedom of India was a subordinate one, were to inculcate in the masses the spirit of nonviolence and to bring about unity between the Hindus and Muslims by a change of heart. He failed miserably in both and realized it only too well at the fag end of his life. The cult of nonviolence never took root in the hearts of the people. Even during the lifetime of Gandhi it was definitely abandoned by new leaders like Jayaprakash Narayan[2] in 1942, and it has not played any role in Indian

politics ever since even under the stewardship of the devoted followers of Gandhi. As regards communal relations Gandhi began his political career by forging the closest bond of amity and cooperation between the Hindus and the Muslims such as had never been witnessed before. But it suffered a complete metamorphosis within a few years, and before Gandhi passed away he had the mortification to witness bitter hatred and hostility between the two communities growing from bad to worse every day — unprecedented in the annals of Indian history after the end of Muslim rule. The failure of his life's task was emphasized by a series of contests between the two communities, accompanied by the most horrible deeds of cruelty of a brutal nature, as if there was a fight between two savage races capable of no thought but that, regardless of all considerations of justice or mercy, their enemies should be exterminated.

The failure of Gandhi to achieve his two great ideals was almost inevitable. In the first case he did not make due allowance for human nature, as it is and always has been. As regards the second, he accepted, as fact, a purely imaginary fraternity, and completely ignored the fundamental differences between the Hindus and Muslims based on history, culture and tradition to which frequent reference has been made in these volumes. But though he failed, his earnest and lifelong devotion to these two noble causes evokes our highest admiration, and his precept and example will always be stored as priceless treasures in India. He should not be judged merely by the result of his actions, but the high motive that inspired him should also be taken into account.

The failure to achieve the two great ideals of nonviolence and Hindu-Muslim unity led to the failure of Gandhi's third ideal, namely, to maintain the political unity of India. For the cult of violence and communal strife were mainly responsible for the creation of Pakistan. As usual, Gandhi held fast to his ideal almost till the last,

[2] Jayaprakash Narayan, a leader of the socialist wing of the Congress, escaped from jail in November 1942 and proceeded to organize anti-British revolutionary activities until he was rearrested in 1943. [Editor's note]

when his dream of a united India was rudely shattered by the action of his own followers. The tragedy of Gandhi's life was that these members of his inner council, who followed him for more than twenty years with unquestioned obedience, took the fatal steps leading to the partition of India without his knowledge, not to speak of his consent. Pyarelal mournfully observes:

Such a thing would have been inconceivable in olden days. Even when he was ranging over the length and breadth of India they did not fail to consult him before taking any vital decision.

Whether Gandhi was right and his followers wrong, does not concern us here. But it certainly shows that reason ultimately took the place of blind faith and devotion to Gandhi. . . .

I have not said much about the Moderate Party after its leaders left the Congress in 1918. . . . The Moderate leaders did not play any significant role in the movement or struggle for freedom as it shaped itself after 1918. The Moderate leaders, however, contend that their policy of co-operation under the new Reform scheme [the Montagu-Chelmsford Reforms of 1919] considerably helped the cause of freedom, and, if sincerely and earnestly followed by the country as a whole, would not have been less fruitful than the policy that was actually pursued.

This raises a controversial issue, namely, whether the achievement of freedom would not have been equally facilitated by following some method other than that pursued by the Congress under the leadership of Gandhi. Such hypothetical questions are always difficult to answer. But it is possible to argue that equal, if not greater, success could have been attained by following the policy of responsive cooperation initiated by Tilak and accepted by Gandhi till the end of 1919. Its essence was to accept and work the reforms that were offered, and carry on mass agitation for more and

more till the goal was attained. In the circumstances created by the Second World War this procedure would have gained enormous strength and could scarcely have failed in the long run. Whether this process would have involved greater delay nobody can definitely say. But, according to a school of thought, it is very likely that the transfer of power under this process would have been far more smooth and the partition of India, with all its attendant horrors, might, *perhaps*, have been avoided. In any case, they say, it would have saved India from the troubles and evils which necessarily resulted from the sudden transfer of power to the hands of a Party organization without any experience of administration. . . . A gradual transfer of power, i.e., transformation of the Executive and the Legislature by systematic grant of more and more power to the elected representatives of the people, was neither theoretically absurd nor an impracticable proposition. But these speculations are at present of little practical value and may be safely left to the verdict of history in future.

* * *

The rise of the Gandhi cult . . . has obscured men's vision about true history. It will be my endeavour to examine some of the fundamental issues involved in forming a proper assessment of the role played by Gandhi, so that the way may be cleared for future historians to deal with this important phase of Indian history in the right spirit. It is obviously impossible to deal with all the aspects of Gandhi's life and activities; so I shall have to concentrate my attention upon a few topics only — specially those in respect of which a reverence for Gandhi has stood in the way of ascertaining the truth. I would attempt to remove the debris and clear the deck.

Gandhi himself often laid stress on three things: the *charka* or spinning wheel, denunciation of violence as a political method, and Hindu-Muslim unity. Of these the first need not be seriously dis-

cussed, for it is now being gradually realized that apart from sentiment it has
played no significant part in the struggle
for India's political or economic independence. It now survives only as a relic of the
Gandhi cult, and it is no use killing a dead
horse.

The cult of *ahimsa* preached by Gandhi,
and the current belief that it alone has
brought independence to India, have stood
in the way of a proper judgment of the
nature of militant nationalism . . . and
the role it played in the struggle for freedom. . . .

* * *

In Western countries perpetrators of political murders are not denounced, but regarded as heroes, and if they are caught
and executed, they are looked upon as
martyrs. Matthew Arnold, in a fine poem,
has distinguished murder for private gain
or hatred from that done for some great
public cause. When, in 1906, some Rus-
sians were assassinated by the Nihilists,
the *Pioneer* of Allahabad wrote:

The horror of such crimes is too great for
words; and yet it has to be acknowledged, almost, that they are the only method of fighting
left to a people who are at war with despotic
rulers able to command great military forces,
against which it is impossible for the unarmed
populace to make a stand.

Such commendations of political violence
may be multiplied to any extent. But Englishmen followed a different standard of
judgment when Indians were concerned.
Mrs. Annie Besant, for example, who denounced Aurobindo as fanatical, wrote as
follows in her unregenerate days:

Violence is the recognized way in England
of gaining political reforms. There would be
no Home Rule Bill if landlords had not
been shot — no Reform Bill of 1832 without
riot and bloodshed.

The revolutionaries in India justified their
deeds on exactly the same grounds as were
advanced by Mrs. Besant and the *Pioneer*.

It will perhaps be news to many that
eminent political leaders, both in England
and India, did not fail to note the value
of the terrorist cult in a freedom movement. When Madan Lal Dhingra shot
dead Sir Curzon Wyllie in 1909, Lloyd
George expressed highest admiration of his
patriotism, and Churchill shared the view.
So far as Indian leaders were concerned,
we have now the evidence of the revolutionaries to the effect that their action was
approved and encouraged by men like Aurobindo Ghose, Surendranath Banerji, As-
wini Kumar Dutta, P. C. Ray, Lajpat Rai
and Bal Gangadhar Tilak.[3] Popular approval of these acts is still to be found in
the folk songs about the martyrs in Bengal
and other parts of India. In the face of all
these it is hardly just to describe the so-
called Terrorist Movement as the product
of a few misguided youths. It was a great
political movement, based upon European
models, and sanctified by the blood, sacrifice and suffering of hundreds of Indian
youths, whose love for their motherland
was proved by the supreme test — the one
touchstone of real love — namely readiness
to die for the object of love. Their martyrdom often touched the sublime.

It is a moot point to decide how far this
method contributed to the success in the
struggle for freedom. . . . The revolutionaries had two main objects in view.
First, to awaken, by a rude shock, the inert
mass of Indians from the political torpor
of ages, and create a revolutionary mentality among the people; secondly, to para-
lyze, as far as possible, the effective work
of administration, and to serve as a perpetual reminder of seething discontent of
the Indians against the British rule. These
objects were achieved to a large extent. Its
indirect effect was also highly important.
With the spread of revolutionary ideas
large bands of young men — even those
who did not actively participate in the revolutionary movement — were imbued with

[3] Some of the most important nationalist leaders
of the time. [Editor's note]

a new spirit of dedicating themselves to the service of the country at the cost of any suffering or sacrifice. Unless this background were prepared, thousands would not have rallied round Gandhi in 1920, when he had just begun his political career in India. In fact some of the ex-terrorists were his most energetic lieutenants.

Further, it is also legitimate to hold, from such evidence as we possess, that the revolutionary activities had a great effect upon the British government, and the Reforms of 1909 and the [Montagu] declaration of 1917 were largely influenced by them. . . .

Today when it has been a fashion to attribute the achievement of independence to nonviolent methods of Gandhi, militant nationalism has come to be looked upon as an evil in itself, and a useless evil at that. I am sure the verdict of history will be very different, and militant nationalism will be accorded its due place among the factors that contributed to our national independence. To this we shall revert later. We may now turn to the next topic, the Muslim nationalism.

*   *   *

Gandhi's handling of the Hindu-Muslim problem profoundly affected the course of struggle for independence. His anxiety for the Hindu-Muslim unity deserves all praise, but his was a sentimental approach to the problem and was not based on a realistic appreciation of the situation. He perhaps thought that by the magic of his nonviolence he would provide synthesis where none appeared possible. He does not appear to have understood the fundamental differences that separated the Muslims from the Hindus, and were too deep to be healed merely by slogans of friendship and fraternity. He failed to understand the real cause of tension between the two communities, because he did not study the problem in its true historical perspective. He shared the common views of the Hindu political leaders that the communalistic outlook of the Muslims blocked the progress of Indian nationalism which they

held out as a great and noble ideal. But the Hindus forgot that while it is easy to follow a noble ideal when it also subserves your material interest, it is more difficult to accept it when, instead, it involved sacrifice and sufferings. Independence of India would give the majority community all the power and prestige, and the minority would be at their mercy. The Muslims could not forget that not long ago they were masters of the Hindus. To be subject to the British was bad enough, but subjection to Hindu domination would be far worse. Such a mentality may be regarded as ignoble from the higher standpoint of nationality, but it is difficult to say that it is unnatural. The Hindu leaders, however, conveniently ignored this point of view altogether. Like them Gandhi also believed that most of the Muslim leaders were inspired by the lofty sentiments of nationalism. . . .

Resentment against the British for their treatment of Turkey . . . drew the Indian Muslims towards the Hindus. Muhammad Ali, who had openly proclaimed that he was a Muslim first and an Indian afterwards, sought for the help and support of Gandhi in this crisis for Turkey, and Gandhi readily agreed. Whatever one might think of his decision to take the leadership in a campaign with which India had no direct concern, his approach to the Khilafat question certainly appears to be very puzzling, not to put it more bluntly.

In his letter to the Viceroy he wrote that the safety of the British Empire depends upon the just treatment of the Khilafatist demand and of the Indians' claim to Home Rule. In other words, he attached equal importance to the independence of India and satisfaction of the claims of Indian Muslims regarding the integrity of the Khilafat in Turkey. Nay, more, he even gave priority to Muslim claim; for he invoked his *Brahmastra,* or the most potent weapon, namely *satyagraha,* for the first time, not for the Home Rule of India, nor for the redress of Punjab atrocities, but for enforcing the Muslim demands, the other two items being added later, on second and third thoughts. If we remember that no other Muslim country in the world was prepared to sacrifice an iota of its national interest for the sake of Khilafat, and that Turkey herself a few years later abolished the Khilafat as a useless appendage to Turkish sovereignty, Gandhi's backing of the Muslim claim, even to the extent of giving it priority over Home Rule, baffles all rational explanation.

Gandhi is reported to have said, in his justification, that such a chance of winning over the Muslims would never come in a hundred years' time. This does little credit either to the head or heart of Gandhi. To seriously think that the policy of a European coalition towards Turkey could be modified by *satyagraha* in India, implies ignorance of European politics, though some would like to call it "a rare sense of expediency sharpened by a sense of his own apostolic power." An alternative hypothesis is to suppose that Gandhi deliberately encouraged the Muslims in a fruitless and hopeless task for the sake of promoting the political interests of the Hindus. But such an attitude is unthinkable in the case of Gandhi. It has been suggested by some that "Gandhi was always capable of working himself up to a Messianic zeal, as an instrument of God; and in such cases Messianic zeal is known to be harnessed to a desire to work miracles." Miracles may happen in the world. But they do not constitute a proper subject of historical inquiry, and should not form the basis of political judgment.

Further, to believe that any effort to help the Muslims on this occasion would forever secure the Hindu-Muslim unity, only betrays a lack of full knowledge regarding the growth of Muslim nationalism. . . . Muhammad Ali laughed at the idea that the Muslims would make matters up with the Hindus because something happened to Muslims outside India, and very pertinently asked, "Have the questions that really divide the two communities lost their force and meaning? If not, then the problem remains exactly where it was at any time in recent Indian history." This is the realistic point of view. To think that a temporary palliative over a side-issue, having no relation to India, would solve the long-standing problem was an absurd idea, to say the least of it.

But there is a far more serious objection to Gandhi's policy. Howsoever opinions might differ as to the basic elements that constitute a nationality, there is a consensus of opinion in one respect. Different groups of people living together cannot constitute a nation unless they have common sympathy, agreement, and interest to an extent, such as does not subsist between any one of them and any nation outside these groups. If a hundred million Muslims in India feel more vitally interested in the welfare of Turkey and other Muslim States outside India, than that of India herself, they can hardly be regarded as a unit of the Indian nation. Gandhi failed to realize that the pan-Islamic movement in India, which he chose to lead, cut at the very root of Indian nationality. By his own admission that the Khilafat question was a vital one for Indian Muslims, even more vital than Home Rule for India, Gandhi himself, put a seal of approval to the oft-repeated claim of Indian Muslims that they formed a separate nation, that they were in India but not of India.

After having cut at the very root of Indian nationalism, by recognizing the Muslims, for all political purposes, as forming a separate nation . . . in 1919, Gandhi and his followers made a complete *volte-face* in 1937. When Jinnah, one of the few real nationalists among the Muslims at one time, suggested a coalition Ministry of the Congress and the Muslim League, the Congress assumed a lofty tone of undiluted Indian nationalism, and refused to entertain any proposal that might have the appearance of representing the Muslims as a separate political unit. The Congress virtually refused to form a coalition ministry with the Muslims unless they liquidated the Muslim League and repudiated all vestiges of their claim to form a separate political entity. Nobody who had any knowledge of the background of Muslim politics could imagine for a moment that the Muslim League would commit political *hara-kiri* at the bidding of the Congress.

It was a momentous decision, probably inspired by belated recognition of what true nationalism demands. But this sense dawned upon the Hindu leaders too late. . . . Jinnah now finally realized that the Muslims, as a separate community, had no political prospects in India. They had no chance of sharing political power with the Hindus; they must either surrender their individuality or cut themselves adrift from the Hindus. The Congress ultimatum was thus the signal for the parting of the ways which, by inevitable stages, led to Pakistan. All proposals for amicable settlement on the basis of the partition of India were violently denounced, and Gandhi held to the last that the partition could only be effected over his dead body. But at last the doctrinaire yielded to the realist. Gandhi had evidently hoped against hope to work a miracle by his nonviolence. But Jinnah's "Direct Action" proved a more effective weapon for achieving independence than *satyagraha*. Violence triumphed over nonviolence.

We may next consider how far nonviolent *satyagraha*, which failed to impress Jinnah, triumphed over the British. According to the current view, this new technique, invented by Gandhi, drove the English, bag and baggage, from India. Let us now examine this claim in a dispassionate spirit, by examining the role played by Gandhi in the struggle for India's freedom.

*   *   *

The aim of *satyagraha*, we are told, is the conversion of the opponent by self-suffering. How it triumphs over the opponent is thus described:

It involves self-chosen suffering and humiliation for the resisters. If it is effective, it is so by working on the conscience of those against whom it is being used, sapping their confidence in the exclusive rightness of their case, making their physical strength impotent, and weakening their resolution by insinuating a sense of guilt for the sufferings they have a part in causing.

Before we proceed further to find out how far the ideal of *satyagraha* was followed in right spirit by the Indian fighters, we may examine the case from the other side. Is there anyone who would seriously claim that Gandhi's *satyagraha* produced the desired or expected effect upon the British and forced them to quit India? Would any rational man believe that Attlee, far less Churchill, or the British people were so much overwhelmed by a sense of guilt for the sufferings they caused in India, that their resolution to keep India under their control was weakened or shaken? Their physical strength, no doubt, deteriorated, but that was due to the hammering blows of Hitler, victories of Japan, and the impossibility of placing reliance on Indian *sepoys* after the formation of the Indian National Army. There is no evidence that *satyagraha* or self-suffering of Gandhi's followers had anything to do with it. Thus according to the accepted interpretation of *satyagraha* it could not have any effect on the British decision to grant independence to India.

We have next to consider the question of *satyagraha* from the Indian side. It has been repeatedly emphasized by Gandhi that nonviolence forms the very basis of *satyagraha*. It is not merely abstaining from violent action, but a complete transformation of life. It is thus expounded by Gandhi.

When a person claims to be non-violent, he is expected not to be angry with one who has injured him. He will not wish him harm, he will wish him well; he will cause him no physical hurt. Thus non-violence is complete innocence.

Gandhi himself admitted in 1930, after more than ten years' experience, that few, if any, of his followers have understood the principles of *satyagraha* or have developed necessary strength to exercise it. Anyone conversant with human nature would hardly expect anything else. But what is worse still, few even among his chief disciples or followers, really believed in the ideal of *satyagraha*. We have recorded evidence that Pandit Motilal Nehru and Jawaharlal Nehru, Maulana Abul Kalam Azad, and many others, had no faith in the creed of nonviolence, though they accepted it as a policy suitable to the circumstances. Gandhi himself knew this quite well, for he said: "If India possessed the sword, I know that India would not have listened to this gospel" of nonviolence.

It is thus quite clear that whatever we might think of the virtue of *satyagraha*, as a principle, it was never really put to the test. It may be doubted whether there were even four hundred real *satyagrahis* out of the 400 millions of Indians. There was thus no real *satyagraha* campaign in India, and of course, no effect of it upon Britain.

On April 20, 1940, after Gandhi's last mass *satyagraha* campaign was over, he wrote in the *Harijan*:

We in India have never given non-violence the trial it deserves. The marvel is that we have attained so much even with our mixed non-violence.

These words deserve most careful consideration. Gandhi himself admits that whatever success he achieved was attained, not by nonviolence, pure and simple, as demanded by *satyagraha,* but by a mixture of violence and nonviolence. This ought to be a corrective to those who today cry hoarse over the discovery of a new technique of nonviolence by which India attained independence, and which should therefore be followed by other countries of the world. As a matter of fact it is held by many that the humane way of British imperialism was mainly responsible even for the limited success of the movement.

Some devoted disciples of Gandhi openly admit that real *satyagraha* was never tried in India, but argue that even the "limited acceptance of *satyagraha*," i.e., the mixed nonviolence of Gandhi, was enough to lead to ultimate victory.

The phrase "limited acceptance of *satyagraha*" is not very easy to understand as an abstract expression. But what it really means is obvious. Gandhi himself referred to non-cooperation and civil resistance (evidently the same as civil disobedience) as the two offshoots of *satyagraha*. To these movements evidently the followers of Gandhi ascribe his ultimate victory. It is, therefore, necessary to examine the validity of this claim.

The non-cooperation movement was formally started in 1921. There is no doubt that it had a very wide response all over the country, betokening a general mass-awakening, the extent and intensity of which was a revelation, both to the people and to the government. But the credit for this cannot go to Gandhi alone. Not even two years had passed since he had seriously entered into Indian politics and emerged as a leader. It is impossible to imagine that during this short period he could convert an inert mass into an active body all over this vast subcontinent. We must hold that the ground was prepared by the great national movement, including its militant aspect, during the preceding sixteen years. The *Swadeshi* movement, starting in Bengal but gradually spreading to distant regions, and the Home Rule movement of Tilak and Besant, based upon mass contact, leavened the common people with a political consciousness unknown before. Gandhi admitted that the Home Rule League workers had prepared the ground in Gujarat, and the same thing was true of other places. The militant nationalism kept alive before the people the ideals of extreme sufferings and supreme self-sacrifice for the cause of the country, which political movements alone could not impart. The cumulative effect of these, and other causes such as the miseries of the people and growing discontent against the government, prepared the ground for a vast mass upsurge such as India never saw before, at least after the outbreak of 1857. No sober historian would perhaps deny the influence of these predisposing causes, and hold that Gandhi alone, by his precepts and exertions, created this mass awakening all over this great subcontinent in less than two years' time during which he was preoccupied by many political affairs.

On the other hand, it is impossible to minimise the importance of the role played by Gandhi. No one without his personality and saintly character would have inspired that confidence and created the will and enthusiasm which alone could galvanize the masses into action. The saint has always had a profound appeal to the Indian mind. It is the great credit of Gandhi — perhaps unique in the world's history — that he could exploit the spirit of devotion and complete self-surrender, usually reserved for a spiritual *Guru,* for political purposes. Dhangopal Mukherji tells us that when, in 1930, he asked the captain of the Bombay Youth League to explain why they followed Gandhiji, he replied as follows:

Gandhi is now marching as Buddha marched through India. . . . When you walk with him a light seems to emanate from him and fills you with its deep radiance. It is a new phenomenon, the present incarnation of Gandhi.

This man blurted out the secret of Gandhi's influence over the masses. It was not the politician but the saint Gandhi, a new incarnation of Buddha, to whom the people's faith and reverence were pledged.

While the common man was attracted by the saintly character of Gandhi, the intellectuals were drawn round him by his magnetic personality. This would be evident from the following confession of Pandit Jawaharlal Nehru.

In spite of the closest association with him (Gandhi) for many years, I am not clear in my own mind about his objective. I doubt if he is clear himself. One step is enough for me, he says; and he does not try to peep into [the] future or to have a clearly conceived end before him.

Why in spite of this Nehru accepted his lead he thus explains:

How came we to associate ourselves with Gandhiji politically and to become, in many instances, his devoted followers? The question is hard to answer. . . . Personality is an indefinable thing, a strange force that has power over the souls of men, and he possesses this in an ample measure. . . . He attracted people. . . . They did not agree with his philosophy of life, or even with many of his ideals. Often they did not understand him. But the action that he proposed was something tangible. . . . Any action would have been welcome after the long tradition of inaction which our spineless politics had nurtured; brave and effective action with an ethical halo about it had an irresistible appeal . . . and we went with him although we did not accept his philosophy.

Pandit Nehru has put, in a nutshell, the best and most reasonable explanation of the secret of Gandhi's unique leadership. It was not his philosophy or ideals, statesmanship or political wisdom and acumen, but the magnetic personality that attracted the intellectual class, including even the highest leaders.

So it is the saintliness and personality of Gandhi that made him dominate Indian politics, and enabled him to launch the campaigns of non-cooperation and civil disobedience, involving mass upsurge on an unprecedented scale. The detailed account of the non-cooperation campaign of 1921 leaves no doubt that Gandhi, the saint, had succeeded, at least for the time being, in instilling into the hearts of the people of India, courage and manhood, discipline and endurance, the spirit of sacrifice for the cause of India's freedom from foreign yoke, and above all, a grim determination to achieve it at any cost. But Gandhi, the politician, hopelessly blundered. He sounded the order of retreat just when the public enthusiasm had reached the boiling point. Even his principal lieutenants like C. R. Das, Motilal Nehru and Lajpat Rai shared the strong general resentment against Gandhi's decision, and regarded it as almost a national calamity. Judged by all rational standards, Gandhi committed a great tactical blunder, leading to deplorable consequences in the political situation of India, particularly in respect of Hindu-Muslim relations.

* * *

The next great movement of Gandhi, which also proved to be his last, was the civil disobedience movement of 1930 which, with a slight break, continued nominally till 1934. In spite of the curious character of his preliminary correspondence with the Viceroy, which was a puzzle even to Nehru, Gandhi's march to Dandi must be admired as a grand conception, superbly executed with a consummate skill. The movement called forth unique examples of patient suffering on the part of a number of men who followed the instructions of Gandhi to the letter. The memorable salt-raid at Dharasana, of which a vivid picture has been given by an American eye-witness,[4] has an epic grandeur of its own, and shows at its very best what the reverence for Gandhi, the saint, could accomplish. But Gandhi, the politician, proved as great a failure in this second campaign, as in the first. It is hard to defend his pact with Irwin on any rational ground, unless it were a tacit admission of failure and inability to continue the civil disobedience movement any further. It is harder still to understand why the great movement, which was declared by Gandhi himself to be a fight to a finish, was suddenly abandoned for the sake of the comparatively minor issue of separate electorate for the depressed classes. Pandit

Jawaharlal Nehru echoed the voice of the country when he said:

I felt annoyed with him (Gandhi) for choosing a side-issue for the final sacrifice. . . . After so much sacrifice and brave endeavour, was our movement to tail off into something insignificant? I felt angry with him at his religious and sentimental approach to a political question, and his frequent references to God in connection with it.

As Gandhi himself disclaimed all responsibility for the violent outbreak in 1942, the suspension of the civil disobedience movement in 1933 practically brings to an end his leadership in the active struggle for freedom on the basis of limited acceptance of *satyagraha,* i.e., nonviolent noncooperation and civil disobedience. A review of the two great campaigns of Gandhi recalls to our mind the observations of C. R. Das. "The Mahatma," said he, "opens a campaign in a brilliant fashion; he works it up with unerring skill; he moves from success to success till he reaches the zenith of his campaign — but after that he loses his nerve and begins to falter." The truth of this remark, which was based on the 1921–22 campaign, was well illustrated by the subsequent campaigns of 1930 and 1932.

What was the net result of these campaigns? It is impossible to describe them here in detail, but reference should be made to two great contributions that they made to India's struggle for freedom. In the first place, the Congress movement had become a real mass movement, and national awakening had extended to the people at large. Secondly, the Congress was turned into a genuine revolutionary organization. These undoubtedly spelt the doom of British domination in India, sooner or later. There is, however, no basis for the claim that the civil disobedience movement directly led to independence. It is opposed to both reason and facts. The campaigns of Gandhi, a mixture of violence and nonviolence, came to an ignoble end about

[4] The reference is to the account of the United Press correspondent, Webb Miller, in his book *I Found No Peace* (New York, 1936), pp. 192–196. [Editor's note]

fourteen years before India achieved independence. They no doubt went a great way in creating an urge for freedom and a grim resolve to achieve it, on the part of the masses. But as the militant nationalism prepared the ground for Gandhi's success in 1921, it also materially contributed to the achievement of freedom. During the First World War the Indian Revolutionaries sought to take advantage of the German help in the shape of war materials to free the country by armed revolt. But the attempt did not succeed. During the Second World War Subhas Bose followed the same method and created the I.N.A. [Indian National Army]. In spite of brilliant planning and initial success the violent campaigns of Subhas Bose failed, like Gandhi's nonviolent campaigns, to achieve freedom. The battle for India's freedom was also being fought against Britain, though indirectly, by Hitler in Europe and Japan in Asia. None of these three scored any direct success, but few would deny that it was the cumulative effect of all the three that brought freedom to India. In particular the revelations made by the I.N.A. trial, and the reaction it produced in India, made it quite plain to the British, already exhausted by the War, that they could no longer depend upon the loyalty of the sepoys for maintaining their authority in India. This had probably the greatest influence upon their final decision to quit India.

I do not propose to discuss in detail the part played by Gandhi during the Second World War and the subsequent period. For it does not appear to have directly helped the advance of India towards freedom. Gandhi, however, rose to high stature as a humanitarian. He wrote to Hitler in 1941 about the soul-force discovered by him and earnestly requested him to desist from war. He wrote two open letters to the British people appealing to them that they should not fight Hitler with arms but oppose him by spiritual force, and interviewed the Viceroy to bring him round to this view. The parties addressed were as much or as little impressed as the Indian leaders were by his proposal on May 24, 1942, that the British and Allied forces should quit India, leaving him to resist the invading Japanese with stubborn nonviolent non-cooperation, as well as his advice to the Viceroy, Lord Mountbatten, that the communal deadlock should be solved by giving Jinnah the sole authority to form a Cabinet, whose members might be all Muslims. These instances are cited to show that while Gandhi will live in history as one of the greatest apostles of peace and nonviolence in a war-stricken world, the credit now given to him for his political acumen which led the Indians to the final victory, cannot command immediate assent, and needs a great deal of objective thinking.

Gandhi and the British Commonwealth

S. R. MEHROTRA

In the reading which follows, S. R. Mehrotra argues that Gandhi's stead-
fast purpose was to maintain close and friendly relations between Britain and
India. His interpretation offers an interesting contrast to that of R. C. Majumdar
in the preceding selection. It was implicit in Majumdar's argument that the purpose of Indian nationalism was to win independence from England as promptly
as possible, by whatever means would prove most effective. By this test, Majumdar found Gandhi to be "lacking in both political wisdom and political strategy." To Mehrotra, in contrast, Gandhi's leadership was successful precisely
because he was able to prevent Indian nationalism from taking a more radical
turn than it did.

GANDHI: THE LOYALIST

Mohandas Karamchand Gandhi learnt his politics in South Africa where he stayed from 1893 to 1914. Like most English-educated Indians of his generation, he was then a loyal and moderate nationalist. He had a romantic veneration for the British constitution, especially because it recognised the principles of individual freedom and racial equality. He was "a lover" of the British Empire, because he thought it was on the whole doing good to his country. He believed that Indians could rise to their full stature within and with the help of the Empire. He wanted his countrymen to qualify for equal partnership in the Empire by loyal service and sacrifice. He himself served with distinction in the Boer War and the Zulu rebellion on the side of the English. In his book *Hind Swaraj*, published in 1909, Gandhi vigorously supported the ideals and methods of moderate Congressmen in India and denounced those of the extremists. Though extremely critical of many aspects of Western civilization, Gandhi genuinely loved the English people and admired the outstanding qualities of their character.

Throughout World War I Gandhi labored strenuously in the cause of the defense of the Empire. He preached "absolutely unconditional and wholehearted co-operation with the government on the part of educated India" in the war effort and emphasised what he considered to be the elementary truth that if the Empire perished, with it would perish their cherished political aspirations for their own country. He disappointed Mrs. Annie Besant in 1915 when he refused to join her in launching a Home Rule movement in India. He told her in so many words that he did not share her distrust of the English people and would do nothing which might embarrass them during the war. He would have liked his countrymen to "withdraw all the Congress resolutions, and not whisper 'Home Rule' or 'responsible government' during the pendency of the war." The Secretary of State, Edwin Montagu, while in India in 1917, noted in his *Diary* after an interview with Gandhi:

(Gandhi) does not understand details of schemes. He wants the millions of India to leap to the assistance of the British throne.

Busy recruiting soldiers for the war, Gandhi wrote to the Viceroy, Lord Chelms-

From S. R. Mehrotra, "Gandhi and the British Commonwealth," *India Quarterly*, XVII (January–March, 1961), 44–55. By permission of the Indian Council of World Affairs.

ford, in April 1918 that he loved the English nation and wished to evoke in every Indian the loyalty of Englishmen. To M. A. Jinnah, who was then engaged, along with Mrs. Besant and B. G. Tilak, in popularising the gospel of Home Rule, he wrote in July 1918: "Seek ye first the recruiting office and everything will be added unto you."

In spite of the ill-timed Rowlatt Act and the unfortunate Amritsar incident, Gandhi pleaded with his people to work the reforms of 1919 in a spirit of genuine cooperation and good will. At the Amritsar session of the Congress held towards the end of December 1919, the latter-day apostle of non-cooperation would not even brook the idea of grudging acceptance or Irish obstructionism which some of the radicals contemplated practising in the councils.

THE LOYALIST TURNS REBEL

It was the events of the next few months which turned the great loyalist and cooperator into a rebel and a non-cooperator. The terms of the Treaty of Sèvres with Turkey, published in May 1920, were considered by most Indians — not only by Muslims — as a breach of earlier solemn pledges given by British statesmen. The Report of the Hunter Commission appeared to them as an attempt to whitewash the culprits in the Amritsar massacre. The manner in which General Dyer's action was acclaimed by a strong element in the House of Commons and a majority in the House of Lords, and the immense public subscription raised for him filled Indians with pain and indignation. Gandhi pleaded with the authorities to put themselves morally right, but the latter failed to appreciate the moral aspect of the issues involved until it was too late. Gandhi became convinced that "the present representatives of the Empire" had become "dishonest and unscrupulous," that they had no real regard for the wishes of the Indian people and counted the honor of India as of little consequence. To an enraged and aggrieved

people he suggested the way of nonviolent non-cooperation to enforce the national will and secure redress of the *Khilafat* and the Punjab wrongs.

Gandhi's movement of nonviolent non-cooperation, launched in August 1920, was more in the nature of an appeal to the English conscience. Gandhi knew that the English were, of all people, peculiarly vulnerable to this weapon. "An Englishman," he told C. F. Andrews, "never respects you till you stand up to him. Then he begins to like you. He is afraid of nothing physical; but he is mortally afraid of his own conscience, if you ever appeal to it and show him to be in the wrong. He does not like to be rebuked for wrong-doing at first; but he will think over it, and it will get hold of him and hurt him till he does something to put it right." Gandhi was, in fact, over-sanguine of his success. He expected his *satyagraha* to be a short and swift campaign to which the British would yield. His judgment was basically sound. Had he been a little less honest and scrupulous, or, as some would say, a better politician than he actually was, he would have scored a resounding triumph by the end of December 1921.[1]

Gandhi's movement was not originally directed against the British Empire. He repeatedly claimed during the years 1920–22 that in showing to the Indian people the way of nonviolent non-cooperation in order to ventilate their grievances, he was rendering a greater service to the Empire than any which he had rendered in the past.

SWARAJ WITHIN THE EMPIRE

In December 1920 the Congress revised its creed and declared its object to be "the attainment of *swaraj* by all legitimate and

---

[1] It is generally believed that the Viceroy, Lord Reading, privately offered in December 1921 to grant full responsible government to the provinces immediately and to convene a conference of Indian leaders to discuss other outstanding issues. Gandhi insisted that the *Khilafat* leaders, Mohamed Ali and Shaukat Ali, who were then in jail, should be invited to the proposed conference. The Viceroy refused to do so and withdrew the offer.

peaceful means." Gandhi was the author of the formula and he explained that the Congress was to strive for achieving self-government within the Empire, if possible, and without, if necessary. Personally he felt confident that *swaraj* within the Empire was possible. "I have faith enough in the British people," he wrote in 1921, "to feel that, whilst they will test our determination and strength to the uttermost, they will not carry it to the breaking-point." He defined *swaraj* as "full responsible government on Dominion lines" and "full Dominion Status" for India. On one point, however, Gandhi was insistent: it must be a free and equal partnership and India must have the right to secede. On October 6, 1920 he wrote, "We must have absolute equality in theory and practice and ability to do away with the British connection." "In a free Commonwealth," he remarked in June 1921, "every partner has as much right to retire if the rest go wrong, as it is his duty to remain so long as the rest are faithful to certain common principles."

DOMINION STATUS VS. INDEPENDENCE

The slogan of complete independence outside the British Empire was first raised in India by Aurobindo Ghose and B. C. Pal in 1907, during the days of the anti-partition agitation in Bengal. Its effect was electrifying but short-lived. After 1909 the cry of complete independence had almost died down. Aurobindo retired from politics and Pal became a convert to the idea of Imperial federation. The Home Rulers never contemplated severance of the British connection. Even that stormy petrel, Tilak, did not advocate *swaraj* outside the British Empire. . . . In the latter half of 1920, however, the demand for complete independence outside the British Empire began to gain strength in India. It was encouraged in part by the events which gave birth to the *Khilafat* and non-cooperation movements. It was inspired by the similar demand being made in Egypt and Ireland at the time. But it was

an Englishman, C. F. Andrews, who did the most to popularize it.

In a series of articles and pamphlets, Andrews condemned the idea of self-government for India within the Empire as the product of a subservient mind. He equated the British Empire with racial domination and economic exploitation and told Indians not to delude themselves with the vain hope that they would some day achieve an equal and honourable place within it. India, Andrews said, was a mother country herself and not a daughter nation like the Dominions. Race, religion, language, history and culture — all separated her from Britain and the Dominions; she could never in reality become an integral part of the British Empire, "which must always remain peculiarly and centrally British." Self-government for India within the Empire was, Andrews argued, not only impossible but also undesirable. The British connection would hamper India's natural and healthy growth. It would involve India in Britain's aggressive wars and perpetuate exploitative Western economic interests in the country.

The case for India's independence outside the British Empire was never before or in after years presented with such convincing logic and telling eloquence as it was by Andrews in 1920–21. His preaching made a tremendous impression in India, not least on such alert young minds as that of Jawaharlal Nehru. It failed, however, to convince Gandhi, who claimed to know Englishmen better. Gandhi publicly expressed his dissent from the views of his friend. He rebuked Andrews severely for his lack of faith in the British connection and for putting forward the demand for complete independence outside the Empire which, he said, had done a great deal of mischief in India. When Andrews remarked, "It would almost seem as if you had more faith in my own countrymen than I have myself," Gandhi replied, "That may be true."

Gandhi had a fundamental, moral objection to the demand for independence outside the Empire. He considered such a demand to be unrighteous — indicating a want of faith in God and in human nature. To say that the English would never grant equal partnership to Indians was, he argued, to suggest that the former were incapable of realizing the first principle of cooperation, namely, the brotherhood of man. Nonviolent non-cooperation, Gandhi never ceased to reiterate, was not a programme for the seizure of power, but for the conversion of Englishmen. The English would be converted when Indians developed internal strength. If they remained unconverted it was the failure of Indians, not of the English. In Gandhi's view it was "petulant," "vindictive," and "religiously unlawful" to refuse an equal and honourable partnership with Britain. "India's greatest glory," he told his countrymen, "will consist not in regarding Englishmen as her implacable enemies, fit only to be turned out of India at the first available opportunity, but in turning them into friends and partners in a commonwealth of nations in place of an empire based upon exploitation of the weaker or undeveloped nations and races of the earth and therefore finally upon force."

It was with such arguments that Gandhi tried to shame into silence the radical idealists in India. There can be little doubt that but for Gandhi's determined opposition the Congress — and even the Muslim League — would have gone over to secession and republicanism in 1920–21. When he was in prison (from March 1922 to February 1924) his arguments were used effectively by the moderate and sober leaders of the nationalists to defy the attempts of the "Young Turks" to get the Congress committed to the ideal of complete independence, implying severance of the British connection.

In his presidential address to the Belgaum Congress in December 1924, Gandhi clearly defined his attitude. "The better mind of the world desires to-day," he remarked, "not absolutely independent states warring against one another, but a federation of friendly interdependent states. The consummation of that event may be far off. I want to make no grand claim for our country. But I see nothing grand or impossible about our expressing our readiness for universal interdependence. It should rest with Britain to say that she will have no real alliance with India. I desire the ability to be totally independent without asserting the independence. Any scheme that I would frame, while Britain declares her goal about India to be complete equality within the Empire would be that of alliance and not of independence without alliance." Gandhi urged Congressmen not to insist on independence in each and every case, not because there was anything impossible about it, but because it was wholly unnecessary. "If the British Government," he argued, "mean what they say and honestly help us to equality, it would be a greater triumph than a complete severance of the British connection."

The Balfour Committee Report and General Hertzog's satisfaction with the results of the Imperial Conference of 1926 added strength to Gandhi's elbow. He used it effectively against the separatists when they moved their annual resolution at the 1926 session of the Congress at Gauhati. He told them that between Britain and the Dominions there was a partnership at will on terms of equality and that *swaraj* under Dominion Status implied the right to secede. . . .

PARTNERSHIP WITH GREAT BRITAIN

While Gandhi was busy trying to keep his unruly followers in check, Lord Birkenhead offered the latter a real boon in the form of the Simon Commission of 1927. Amidst the atmosphere of universal indignation aroused in India by the appointment of an exclusively British Commission, the radical idealists, led by Jawaharlal Nehru, found it easy to make the Congress pass a resolution in December 1927 declaring "the goal of the Indian people to be complete national independence." The creed of the Congress, as defined by the constitution of 1920, remained unchanged, but the separatists had now unfurled their banner. Gandhi was very angry. He denounced the resolution as "ill-conceived." "My ambition," he wrote, "is much higher than independence. Through the deliverance of India, I seek to deliver the so-called weaker races of the earth from the crushing heels of Western exploitation in which England is the greatest partner. If India converts, as it can, Englishmen, it can become the predominant partner in a world commonwealth of which England can have the privilege of becoming a partner if she chooses. . . . This is big talk I know. For a fallen India to aspire to move the world and protect weaker races is seemingly an impertinence. But in explaining my strong opposition to this cry for independence, I can no longer hide the light under a bushel. Mine is an ambition worth living for and worth dying for. In no case do I want to reconcile myself to a state lower than the best for fear of consequences. It is, therefore, not out of expediency that I oppose independence as my goal."

Though Gandhi was able to persuade the Congress in December 1928 to accept the ideal of Dominion Status postulated in the All-Parties Conference Report, it was with great difficulty and only on the condition that if the government did not accept the Report within a year the Congress would inscribe the ideal of complete independence on its banner. This condition not being fulfilled, despite Lord Irwin's well-meant efforts, the Congress decided at Lahore in December 1929 to declare complete independence as its goal. The clever Mahatma, however, once again confounded the radicals. The latter were to have nothing but their pound of flesh. Gandhi judged correctly that a refusal to accept the ideal of complete independence would split the Congress over an unreal issue. He himself fully appreciated the nature of Dominion Status and the degree of freedom it im-

plied, but he had to make allowance for the sentiments, the prejudices, and what he called "the inferiority complex" of those who objected to it as an ideal. He therefore decided to satisfy their clamour for complete independence but saw to it that the Congress was not committed to secession. By a formal resolution it was declared that "the word swaraj in the Congress constitution shall mean complete independence." What this complete independence signified was not defined. When Subhas Bose moved an amendment proposing, among other things, the addition of a rider to complete independence "implying thereby complete severance of the British connection," Gandhi vigorously opposed it and the Congress agreeing with him rejected it with an overwhelming majority. Even at that Congress session, Gandhi made it clear that the resolution was not a declaration of independence, nor did it preclude association with Britain on terms of equality. Soon after the Congress session he assured the British that the resolution on complete independence need cause no alarm, "for has it not been admitted by responsible British statesmen that Dominion Status is virtual independence?" In fact, he requested the Viceroy, Lord Irwin, not to play the game of the extremists in India by branding the demand for complete independence as seditious while extolling the glories of Dominion Status. Irwin wrote to King George on 13 March 1931 that it was "definitely untrue to suggest, as I see it suggested that he (Gandhi) is out to break the unity of Your Majesty's Empire." Irwin conveyed to King George what Gandhi had told him, that in his view "the highest form" of complete independence for India was one that could be attained "in association with Great Britain."

At the second Round Table Conference, which he attended, Gandhi made it clear beyond a shadow of doubt that he did "not wish to sever the bond, but to transform it," and that what the Congress demanded was not secession but merely the right to secede. "If we are intent upon complete independence," he remarked, "it is not from any sense of arrogance; it is not because we want to parade before the universe that we have now severed all connection with the British people. Nothing of the kind. On the contrary, you will find . . . that the Congress contemplates a partnership — the Congress contemplates a connection with the British people — but that connection to be such as can exist between two absolute equals."

"Time was," he added, "when I prided myself on being, and being called, a British subject. I have ceased for many years to call myself a British subject; I would far rather be called a rebel than a subject. But I have aspired — I still aspire — to be a citizen, not in the Empire, but in a Commonwealth; in a partnership if possible — if God wills it an indissoluble partnership — but not a partnership superimposed upon one nation by another. Hence you find . . . that the Congress claims that either party should have the right to sever the connection, to dissolve the partnership." As for the words "Dominion Status" or "complete independence," he did not care. "Call it by any name you like," he said, "a rose will smell as sweet by another name, but it must be the rose of liberty that I want and not the artificial product."

Although Gandhi continued to say until 1939 that he would be satisfied with Dominion Status for India, he had, ever since 1931, begun to veer round gradually, almost reluctantly, to the view of Andrews and Jawaharlal Nehru, that the concept of Dominion Status was not applicable to India for the simple reason that India was not a daughter nation. The definition of "Dominion" by enumeration in the Statute of Westminster, the deliberate avoidance of the term "Dominion Status" in the Government of India Act of 1935, and the fact that the British Commonwealth still comprised white members only — all served to deepen this impression. Nor could he fail to note that the vast majority of Indian nationalists was allergic to that idea. When, therefore, during the Second World War, the British Government made offers of Dominion Status to India at the end of hostilities, Gandhi advised them to talk of independence and not of Dominion Status. It was not until 1946 that the British Government appreciated his point. But even when Gandhi became a convert to the idea of independence, he never failed to assert that he visualised nothing but the closest and friendliest relations between an independent India and Great Britain. And inasmuch as the Commonwealth connection was in the Indian mind synonymous with the connection with Great Britain, Gandhi's conversion was not of much consequence.

A FRIENDLY FOE

Gandhi — "the opponent of British rule in India, who yet understood and even loved the English people" — was the strangest rebel the world has ever known. Day in and day out for thirty years, he told his countrymen that they should regard Englishmen as their friends and not enemies, that their fight was against the system and not against the men administering it, and that insofar as they failed to understand this distinction they harmed their own cause. Even a man like Jawaharlal Nehru, who did not stand much in need of such preaching, admitted its corrective effect in his life and thinking. It is rare for a nationalist leader to avow openly and unceasingly that he had been and remained "a sincere friend" of the country against which he was waging a nonviolent war. Nor was it insignificant that his war was nonviolent. Competent English observers have testified that Gandhi, by bringing the Indian revolutionary movement into the open, freed it from secret, terroristic activities and rid the English of the Mutiny complex. Had the Indian nationalist movement turned violent, it would have in its turn invited violent repression, and ended by leaving a legacy of bloodshed, which would have been extremely hard to overcome. If there was no "Mutiny" or "Amritsar" after 1919, and if the transfer of power in India in 1947 could be "a treaty of peace without a war," credit is as much due to Gandhi's leadership as to enlightened British leadership.

Gandhi did not allow Indian nationalism to become narrow, racial and isolationist. He tried his best to save the Congress from getting into the strait jacket of secession and republicanism. He gave it the right leaders. He consistently opposed those who stood for a total break with Britain and advocated the setting-up of a parallel government in India. He forced the separatists in India to argue their case on a high moral level, free from distorting emotion and prejudice. He never looked for outside help to free India. He kept the quarrel between England and India, what it was in essentials, a family quarrel. "I know the English and they know me; ours is a deadly but friendly struggle," he was fond of telling foreigners.

In the final stages of the negotiations which led to the transfer of power in India in 1947, Gandhi did not play a major role, but the settlement on the basis of Dominion Status had his blessings. He called it "the noblest act of the British nation." "The British," he told his prayer audience on 28 September 1947, "rose to the occasion, decided voluntarily to break the empire, and erect, in its place, an unseen and more glorious empire of hearts."

The Communist Reappraisal of Gandhi — I

E. M. S. NAMBOODIRIPAD

The preceding selections by R. C. Majumdar and S. R. Mehrotra illustrated two sharply divergent interpretations of Gandhi's leadership of the Indian nationalist movement. A third way of looking at many of the same questions is that of the Marxists, who seek to explain Gandhi's actions in terms of the political needs of the Indian bourgeoisie or capitalist class. This viewpoint was expressed in the earlier reading from Rajani Palme Dutt. While Indian Communists continue to hold to this general interpretation, in recent years they have tended to display a more appreciative attitude towards Gandhi's total historical role, recognizing not only his contribution to the winning of independence but also his efforts to arouse the social consciousness of India to the problems of its poverty-stricken people. E. M. S. Namboodiripad headed the first Communist government ever to be elected in India when he served from 1957 to 1959 as Chief Minister of the state of Kerala. Under the title The Mahatma and the Ism (1959), Namboodiripad has published an extensive review-essay on D. G. Tendulkar's eight-volume biography, Mahatma, and the first selection below is taken from the concluding section of this essay.

WHAT is the significance of the life and teaching of Mahatma Gandhi? Is the story of his life "the story of his experiments with truth" as he himself put it in the 1920's when he started writing his autobiography?

How are we to explain the evolution of Mohandas Gandhi into the "Father of the

From E. M. S. Namboodiripad, *The Mahatma and the Ism*, 2nd ed. (New Delhi, 1959), pp. 111–117 and pp. ix–xii.

Nation"; the devoted [recruiting] sergeant during the First World War into the leader of the "Do or Die" movement of 1942, with its inspiring slogan of "British Rulers, Quit India"; the scion of a family of loyal servants of the feudal rulers of Porbunder State into a fighter for democracy in the Indian States; the religious-minded youth who was not attracted by any of the radical movements, but landed himself in the Society of Vegetarians in London, into the most outstanding leader of the anti-imperialist and democratic movement in our country? . . .

It is a measure of the enormous significance of the role played by Gandhiji in the history of our national movement that every trend and faction inside the Congress, and almost every political party barring the Communist Party, uses the name of Gandhiji and his teachings for justifying and defending its policies. Serious attempts to assess the role and significance of Gandhiji and his teachings should, therefore, be considered of enormous practical importance for the further development of the democratic movement.

This is not an easy task. Like several other historical personages, Gandhiji had a highly complex personality; his teachings, too, are incapable of oversimplified assessments on the lines of his being "the inspirer of the national movement who roused the masses to anti-imperialist action," "the counterrevolutionary who did all he could to prevent the development of our national movement on revolutionary lines," etc.

His life was so rich in events, his speeches and writings so prolific and touched such varied fields of human activity, his actions at various stages so dramatic, that it will be easy enough for any student of his life and teachings to prove his or her own pet theory about Gandhiji and Gandhism. What he or she has to do is only to string together a series of selected incidents from his life and selected pronouncements from his speeches and writings. It is, however, far more difficult to select those that are really significant from the point of view of history, see the interconnection between the various aspects of his life and teachings, and then to arrive at an integrated understanding of the man and his mission.

Unfortunately for us, the efforts which have so far been made belong to the two categories — either oversimplified and one-sided tributes, or equally oversimplified and one-sided criticisms. Every effort should, therefore, be made to avoid both these pitfalls. It is as a contribution to such efforts that the conclusions which appear to the present writer to flow from his life are given below.

The *first* point to be noted is that Gandhiji was an idealist — idealist not only in the sense that the world-outlook which guided him was opposed to philosophical materialism, but also in the sense that he kept before him certain ideals to which he clung till the end of his life. Moral values like truth, non-violence, renunciation of the pleasures of life, etc.; political ideals such as freedom, democracy, peace, etc.; social objectives such as abolition of caste distinctions, emancipation of women, unity of all national groups and communities, etc. — these were indivisible parts of his life and teachings. It is this adherence to certain ideals that made him plunge into the South African *satyagraha* movement in the early part of his public life; it was this again that enabled him to work out his non-cooperation and other campaigns for the freedom of the nation; it was this that made him the champion of innumerable democratic causes and ultimately made him a martyr in the noble cause of national unity.

Secondly, his idealism played a big role in rousing the hitherto slumbering millions of the rural poor. The semi-religious language which he used in speaking to them, the simple unostentatious life which he led, and the passion with which he fought for their demands — all these drew the millions of the rural poor towards him. They looked upon him as their saviour, as a new incarnation of God, out to deliver them from the miserable plight in which they are placed.

We may well consider his views on several social, economic and cultural questions as "reactionary" (many of them undoubtedly are reactionary). It would, however, be a profound mistake to miss the fact that it was these "reactionary" views of his that enabled him to form a bridge between the mass of peasantry and the sophisticated representatives and leaders of the modern national-democratic movement. It may appear self-contradictory if one were to say that Gandhiji with his "reactionary" social outlook was instrumental in bringing about a profoundly revolutionary phenomenon — the drawing of the mass of the rural poor into the arena of the modern national-democratic movement. This self-contradiction, however, is a manifestation of the contradiction in the real political life of our nation, arising out of the fact that the national-democratic movement was led by the bourgeoisie, linked with feudalism.

Thirdly, it should be pointed out that, though he played a vital role in drawing the mass of the rural poor into the national movement, it would be wrong to ascribe to him personally the tremendous awakening which they showed in the years after the First World War. For, this awakening was the result of historic developments that were taking place in India as well as throughout the world. The slow and steady deterioration in the economic conditions of the Indian peasantry which reached alarming proportions during and immediately after the First World War; the growth of a radical wing inside the Indian national movement, which in certain areas touched sections of the peasantry as well; the impact of such international developments as the Turkish, Chinese and, above all, Russian revolutions on the minds of the Asian people as a whole — these were some of the basic causes which had started acting on the consciousness of the Indian peasantry. They would have acted — probably

not in the same way — even if Gandhiji had not come on the scene.

Stating this is not to deny Gandhiji's role as an individual in giving a specific character to the awakening of the Indian peasantry, to the fact that the new upsurge came to be linked with the political movement for freedom and democracy. To deny Gandhiji's contribution to the drawing of the rural poor and to the consequent strengthening of the national-democratic movement would be as one-sided as to ascribe to him all the credit for the people's awakening itself.

Fourthly, while Gandhiji thus deserves praise for his role in overcoming the major weaknesses of the national-democratic movement — making the movement really national and all-class by bringing in the large masses of the hitherto unorganized rural poor — it should not be forgotten that he had always been and continued till his death to be afraid of the rural poor acting as an independent force. While he was all for mobilizing them in the struggle for freedom and democracy, he was keen that they should act under the leadership of his own class, the bourgeoisie.

Ever since the days of Chauri-Chaura, he had taken special care to devise all manner of measures to see that at every stage in the struggle for freedom and democracy, the rural poor kept themselves within the limits which were considered safe for the bourgeoisie. Anybody who fails to recognize this reality will be unable to explain why he was so insistent on nonviolence being observed by the people in their struggle against imperialism and their agents, while he had no qualms of conscience in acting as the recruiting sergeant for imperialism during the first world war.

Fifthly, not only in relation to the rural poor, but also in relation to the working class and other sections of the working people, his was an approach which, in actual practice, helped the bourgeoisie. His theory of trusteeship, his insistence on certain moral values as the guiding lines for any political activity, the skilful way in which he combined his own extra-parliamentary activities (constructive program and *satyagraha*) with the parliamentary activity of his lieutenants, the characteristically Gandhian way of combining negotiations with the enemy even while carrying on mass direct action against him — all these proved in practice to be of enormous help to the bourgeoisie in (a) rousing the masses in action against imperialism and in (b) preventing them from resorting to revolutionary mass action. This ability of his to rouse the masses and yet to check them, to launch anti-imperialist direct action and yet to go on negotiating with the imperialist rulers made him the undisputed leader of the bourgeoisie. He was a leader in whom all factions and groups inside the class had confidence and who, therefore, could unify and activize it.

Finally, Gandhiji's role in history as the foremost leader of the bourgeoisie should not be taken to mean that he was always, and on every issue, at one with the bourgeoisie. On the other hand, it is characteristic of him, and the class of which he was the friend, philosopher and guide, that, on several occasions and on several issues, his was a minority voice, if not a lone voice. On all such occasions, he and they agreed among themselves that they would temporarily go along different paths. This is a phenomenon which manifested itself again and again — first in the post-non-cooperation years (division of labor between swarajists and no-changers); then in the years after the 1932–33 civil disobedience movement; several times during the Second World War and, finally, in the months preceding and following the attainment of independence.

Particularly was this true of the last days of his life when his idealism came into conflict with the "iron practicalism" of the "steel-minded" Sardar Patel,[1] with the modernism of the radical intellectual Pandit Nehru, and several others who had been his colleagues and lieutenants for several years. It was this growing gulf between him and his colleagues that made his life tragic in the post-independence months, even before that life came to a tragic end.

It is when we examine this growing gulf between him and his colleagues in the last days of his life that we come to a really objective all-sided assessment of Gandhiji, the man and his mission. For this growing gulf was the manifestation of the reality that Gandhiji's insistence on certain moral values had once been helpful to the bourgeoisie, but became, in the last days of his life, a hindrance.

In the days in which it had to fight on two fronts — fight imperialism and, to this end, bring the mass of our urban and rural poor into action; at the same time, fight the trend towards revolutionary action which was growing among the masses — the bourgeoisie found it quite useful to resort to the technique of nonviolent resistance evolved by Gandhiji. However, once the struggle against imperialism was crowned with success, in the sense that the bourgeoisie and its class allies got state power, it was no more necessary to fight a two-front battle. Whatever further struggles have to be waged against imperialism can be waged at the state level, for which it was not necessary to draw the masses of our people into action.

Furthermore, the very fact that the bourgeoisie got state power in its hands and had to use it in its own class interests, brought it and its state machinery into ever more conflicts with the mass of our people. Another result of their coming to power was that the individual representatives of the bourgeoisie who came to power (ministers, MPs, and MLAs, etc.) began to enrich themselves and their friends, relatives, hangers-on, etc., at the cost of the state as well as of the people; to this end, they resorted to any and every corrupt methods provided they yielded results.

[1] Vallabhbhai Patel (d. 1950), one of the main Congress leaders at the time of independence. [Editor's note]

It was this change in the position of the bourgeoisie as a class and its individual representatives that brought it into conflict with Gandhiji, the man who still clung to the ideals which he had been preaching in the days of anti-imperialist struggle. The moral values which he had preached in the days of anti-imperialist struggle now became a hindrance to the politicians who came to power. Gandhiji, on the other hand, remained true to them and could not reconcile himself to the sudden change which occurred in his former colleagues and lieutenants. Particularly was this so on the question of Hindu-Muslim unity and on the corruption in the ranks of the Congress. . . .

We may conclude by saying that Gandhiji became the Father of the Nation, precisely because the idealism to which he adhered in the years of anti-imperialist struggle became a practically useful political weapon in the hands of the bourgeoisie; furthermore, that he became more or less isolated from the bourgeoisie in the latter days of his life, because his idealism did in the post-independence years become a hindrance to the self-interest of the bourgeoisie.

*   *   *

Critics . . . have tried to discover a "contradiction" in my assessment of Gandhiji. I stated on the one hand that he played a big role in rousing the hitherto slumbering millions of the rural poor; on the other hand, I stated that he acted as a leader of the bourgeoisie. Is this not contradictory, they ask?

May I point out in all humility that there is no contradiction in this unless the term "bourgeoisie" is understood to mean merely an epithet of abuse. To say that the class essence of one's approach to problems is bourgeois-democratic, rather than proletarian, is not to say that one's approach to every question is reactionary. A reference to the founders and leaders of Marxism-Leninism will be enough to convince anyone that the bourgeoisie has, in every country, and at a particular stage in the history of its national-democratic movement, acted as a force which roused and organized the mass of the people against reaction — feudal, colonial or both. This role of the bourgeoisie has always been acclaimed and appreciated by Marxist-Leninists who, however, have never failed to point out that this role of the bourgeoisie in rousing and organizing the masses has very serious limitations. While the classical revolutions made by the bourgeoisie — the French Revolution of 1789–1793 — roused and led the mass of French peasantry in a direct onslaught against feudalism, that very same bourgeoisie, in that very same revolution, betrayed the very same peasantry when a particular stage had been reached of that revolution. Basically, the same story was repeated in subsequent bourgeois-democratic revolutions which have been beautifully described in some of the classical works of Marx and Engels (cf. *The Eighteenth Brumaire of Louis Bonaparte, The Class Struggles in France 1848–1850, Germany: Revolution and Counterrevolution, Civil War in France,* etc.).

Lenin too emphasized this dual role of the bourgeoisie in his writings on the national liberation movements in colonial, semi-colonial and dependent countries. Hence it is only those who lack a correct understanding of the role of the bourgeoisie, those who imagine that characterisation of someone as the ideological representative of the bourgeoisie is nothing but a term of abuse, will find in my assessment of the Mahatma a contradiction.

Let me also add that, when I characterised Gandhiji as the ideological representative of the bourgeoisie, I did not at all ascribe to him any motive of protecting the interests of the bourgeoisie. It is a misfortune of every human being that history's verdict of what he or she does is different from what he or she thinks he or she does. Mahatma Gandhi may have honestly believed that he was safeguarding the interests of the entire nation and not of a particular class or community. The point is:

What were the actual results of this practical activity? This applies to lesser individuals as well. A famous saying goes, "The path to hell is paved with good intentions."

It will, of course, be unbalanced if one were to try to assess a person only by the results of his actions; his intentions are also important. As a matter of fact, the correct way of assessing him and his work will be to find out his intentions, the method through which he tried to fulfill them and the results that followed them. This, I claim, is what I have tried to do in this book.

The five-point assessment made by me . . . begins with the statement "that he kept before him certain ideals to which he clung till the end of his life. . . . These were indivisible parts of his life and teachings." Developing the point further, I repeated the same idea: "The moral values which he had preached in the days of anti-imperialist struggle now became a hindrance to the politicians who came to power. Gandhiji, on the other hand, remained true to them and could not reconcile himself to the sudden change which occurred in his former colleagues and lieutenants." It is to this loyalty to certain moral values and ideals which Gandhiji showed down to the end of his life, and to the lack of such loyalty to ideals and moral values on the part of his colleagues, that I trace what I call "the growing gulf between him and his colleagues in the last days of his life." There is, therefore, no question of my attributing any selfish or discreditable motives to Gandhiji. On the contrary, I give him full credit for his idealism.

But, as in the case of such prophets as the Buddha, Jesus, or Mohammed (not to speak of lesser mortals), Gandhiji's ideals and moral values were not mere abstractions; they were part of the great drama of history in which millions upon millions of human beings were involved.

Any one of us (not to speak of such prophets) may have so many ideals which, by themselves, may be good or bad. They would, however, remain with the person who preaches them unless they conform to the vaguely felt desires and requirements of other persons. The larger the circle of people with whose requirements and desires one's ideals conform, the more successful are his preachings and the more popular is the person who preaches them. The Buddha, Jesus and Mohammed were great prophets, precisely because the ideals and moral values to which they clung conformed to the requirements and desires of the millions of human beings, not only in their lifetime but for centuries thereafter.

Gandhiji, too, was great because the ideals and moral values to which he clung to the end of his life conformed to the requirements and desires of the millions of the Indian people. His teachings were for the nation as a whole a call of revolt. Particularly were they a call of revolt to the mass of rural poor, the lowliest of the lowly in the villages, the *Daridranarayans* as he called them. His conception of love, truth, justice, etc., were, in the context of the time, an inspiration for the mass of the rural poor to free themselves from the social, economic and political bonds, which have tied them to imperialism and feudalism. The mass of the rural poor, therefore, looked up to him as a new messiah, their saviour and protector.

It was, however, not only the mass of the rural poor, but other sections of the nation, too, who found in Gandhiji a great man who preached certain ideals and moral values which corresponded to their desires and immediate interests. The Indian working class which had not yet developed its own independent political movement found in him the champion of their interests. The middle-class intelligentsia and youth, fired as they were with the passion to work and fight for something great and noble, found in him an inspiring leader who taught them how to fight for a noble cause and die if need be. Even the well-to-do ladies and gentlemen of the upper classes — the bourgeoisie and the landed gentry — found in him the man who was an ardent patriot working selflessly for a noble cause and, above all, keeping "the mob" within the strict limits of nonviolence.

He, therefore, became the leader of various sections of the people whose desires and requirements naturally varied. Nevertheless, he was able, at least in the beginning, to keep them united under his leadership, since what he had preached gave some sort of satisfaction to all of them. However, as the movement began to advance, these conflicts of the interests and desires of different sections came out into the open. It was this phenomenon that led to conflicts within the organization which he led in the various phases of its history.

Summing up all these conflicts which arose as a result of his leadership in the movement, we come to the conclusion that Gandhiji's idealism had its strong and weak points. His strong points may be summed up in his ability to rouse the masses and organize them in the struggle against imperialism and feudalism; his weak points may be summed up in his insistence on a scrupulous adherence to what is called nonviolence, which, in effect, served to restrain the mass of workers and peasants who want to shake off the triple yoke of imperialism, feudalism and capitalism. This, incidentally, is precisely what the interests of the bourgeoisie demanded. They wanted the mass of our people to be roused and organized against imperialism and feudalism; they, however, wanted these masses to be severely restrained in their actions and struggles. It was this coincidence of what the interests of the bourgeoisie required and the totality of the results of Gandhiji's leadership that is meant when I say that Gandhiji's approach to life and history is a bourgeois-democratic approach.

The Communist Reappraisal of Gandhi — II

HIREN MUKERJEE

Hiren Mukerjee, a professor of history, is also a Communist representative in the Lok Sabha, India's national parliament. The following selection is from his book Gandhiji: A Study (1960).

GANDHI was, indubitably, one of the great social reformers of history. He could not "abolish" untouchability, though the Constitution of India today avers, with a fine indifference to facts, that it has been "abolished." But the jolt which Gandhi, preeminently, gave to that age-old infamy produced cracks and fissures which portend its doom. This alone is achievement enough for a fair-size "great" man, but Gandhi's work was vast and manifold. Even so, this magnificent social reformer hugged certain obvious superstitions. Tagore sharply criticised him for ascribing the terrible Bihar earthquake of 1934 to the sins of the people; in what respects the Biharis had excelled as sinners was not of course explained by him. . . . It is notable that for Voltaire, the great Lisbon earthquake of 1775 finally destroyed the belief that it was possible to justify God's ways to man, but in Gandhi's case the problem did not arise. Not a blade of grass moved, he felt, without God's injunction behind it,

From Hiren Mukerjee, Gandhiji: A Study, rev. ed. (New Delhi, 1960), pp. 191–198. By permission of the author.

and he could only accept a happening and think out a cause according to his lights. This bent of mind affected naturally his politics. To give only one instance, it can be asked why and how it was that with regard to the Muslim problem Gandhi who began so well let things drift so long until India was vivisected. The "vivisection" was "an inglorious end" to three decades of work, the "hollow husk," as Gandhi himself called it, of freedom. Perhaps the only Gandhian answer is that everything rested in God's hands, that Gandhiji could act only in accordance with God's will as he understood it, and leave the rest, even the fruits of the action, as the Gita taught, to God. Such formulations have perhaps a sublime touch but also, in terms of real life, an element of futility and failure. . . .

Speaking of him in relation to the common run of the world's political leaders, somebody once described Gandhi as "an oasis of meditation in our vast and garrulous vacuity." No wonder that, in spite of lacunae, sometimes disturbingly gaping, in his social understanding, he was a whole man, with his mind's gadgets well adjusted, and possessed of a single-mindedness without which achievement is impossible. He was somewhat insensitive to certain human responses to sheer beauty and to works of man's own art . . . but he was in tune with the pulse of a multitudinous, long-suffering people — one of those rare men in face of whom agreement or disagreement, whether about theories or practice, are nearly irrelevant.

To claim, however, as is usually done, that Gandhi was the maker of India's freedom is far from the truth. His contribution to that achievement was, no doubt, very large, but it was not the causative factor. No wide-awake student of history will agree that India could have been free by use of the Gandhian variety of *satyagraha* alone, without the sequence of national effort for at least fifty years and the great post-war upsurge which swept over the country in 1945–46. . . . The people's deviations from the rails of *satyagraha*, rather

than *satyagraha* itself, put fear in the alien administration and made its continuance impossible. This is not to deny the mobilizing role of *satyagraha*, whose call, understood in their own way by the people, roused them to great endeavor. But to claim *satyagraha*'s exclusive potency in the fight for Indian freedom is unhistorical and untrue.

It was perhaps Renan who once said that when Fate could not destroy a great man it sent him disciples in revenge. These disciples, with the exception only of a very few, would perhaps in Gandhi's case have made some sort of a god out of him after his death — a process which had gone pretty far even during his lifetime, a process which, in fairness to Gandhi, it must be said he discouraged. That such deification has not actually taken place is evidence of India's comparative maturity, but what has happened, namely, the ascription alone to Gandhi and his movement of the credit for achievement of Indian freedom shows also that the disciples have tried all the art that they knew to impress the country with their own importance. No one man in the history of India struggling to be free has played as large a part as Mahatma Gandhi, but he did not work on virgin soil and he did not work alone.

In the century between the battle of Plassey (1757) and the Great Revolt of 1857, there never was a time when some region or other in India was not fighting for freedom. "Eighteen-fifty-seven" continues to be the symbol of our people's defiant, if still inchoate, urge for the country's freedom. In the eighteen-seventies, Alan Octavian Hume, "Father of the Congress," discovered . . . that movements for subversion of British rule were more or less active everywhere and could, unless checked in time, coalesce into something fatal to the regime. The last decade of the nineteenth century and the first decade of the twentieth witnessed the first wave of India's recognizably nationalist struggle for freedom, with the *Swadeshi* and "boycott" movement of Bengal in the foreground. It was then, also, that the so-called terrorist wave began, in Bengal, Punjab and elsewhere — a movement often pilloried by moderate constitutionalists and by sticklers for nonviolence, a movement often also blind to the need of the mobilization of our masses in freedom's struggle, but a movement which helped, indubitably, to restore to a morally debilitated people its sense of manhood, to rekindle a new heroism, to give defiant and shining shape to its desire. The example of a Khudiram in 1908, a "Tiger" Jatin in 1916, a Bhagat Singh in 1930,[1] meant something which neither "liberal" constitutionalism nor nonviolent *satyagraha* could bedim in the vision of the people.

Apart from these trends and as a beacon of the future, there was the rising movement of our working people, toilers in factories and in the fields, whose ranks were joined later by "white-collar" employees, growingly conscious as the years passed of their links with the common worker and the unity of their aims. The history of the working-class movement and of its "strike" weapon . . . was a history by no means unrelated to the national struggle for freedom. . . . In 1920–21, 1927–30, 1934–41, and in 1945–47, the upsurge of the working class, supported since the early 'thirties by the growing organization of the peasantry, was a great feature of our national life. Imperialism employed against it all its wiles, besides of course repression, and in the infamous Meerut Conspiracy Case (1929–34)[2] tried at once to decapitate the working class of its leadership and to drive a wedge between the national movement and the working class by lurid denunciations of socialism. In 1945–46 it was clear that while the Congress leadership was keen on restraining the people's advance, the independent movement of the working people swept ahead, but unhappily in the

latter's organization and leadership there were still serious defaults, and it was unable to prevent the emergence of militant and separatist forces of communalism which the bourgeois national leadership could not, on its own, defeat. Even so, it was . . . the great post-war upsurge since late 1945 to which the people's enthusiasm over the "Indian National Army" gave a big impetus, that compelled capitulation of imperialism. That it was only partial is seen in the price that was exacted by imperialism for the transfer of power, the price of partition, of acerbated communal antagonism, of insensate killings and migrations, and of the demoralization that has followed since like an evil taint on our freedom.

Even so acute and occasionally critical a disciple like [J. B.] Kripalani has claimed credit for his master for the achievement of freedom "with such little bloodshed and violence" — credit as much for Gandhi and his movement as for Britain, the generous giver of that freedom! It is a pity that in this connection two very important things are blissfully forgotten. One is that . . . India not having to pay much of a price for her freedom is a myth. Apart from our martyrs unwedded to nonviolence, the process of the transfer of power to deliberately divided India implied, before and after the event and as an inevitable concomitant thereof, an amount of human suffering for millions of people which, in quantity or in quality, is hardly less than the suffering involved in perhaps any of history's great revolutions. The second thing to remember is that, unlike in such revolutions, the suffering borne by the people of India and Pakistan, before and after the constitution of the two states, was at bottom senseless and no spur, at all, to great endeavor. It was a form of massive agony which numbs body and soul and does not release, in the very suffering of it, the heightening qualities of character. One might almost say that we purchased our political freedom with coin that was ethically counterfeit, and so it has been

[1] The individuals mentioned were executed by the British for terrorist activities. [Editor's note]
[2] The trial of thirty-two communist and trade union leaders on charges of conspiring to deprive the king-emperor of his sovereignty over India. [Editor's note]

that even yet our people do not feel sufficiently the glow of that freedom. On August 15, 1947, there came, of course, to our people's minds a great exhilaration — on that day, even in a place like Calcutta, lacerated till the day before by communalism's ugly spears, the countenance of the people, momentarily, was as the sun shineth in his strength. But the mood and the spirit passed — while it could have been lasting if we had won our freedom otherwise than by arrangement with an imperialism which craftily exacted a price which we could not pay without drastic detriment to our soul. This, it bears repetition, should be remembered earnestly, if we wish to understand why even for such forward-looking things as the Plans the hearts of the Indian people yet remain really untouched. The manner we won our freedom — and most of all, it saddened the great Gandhi — has left an unwanted stamp on all that has followed so far.

All this is by no means to belittle Gandhi's achievement, both in regard to the country's freedom and to tasks of social reconstruction. It must not be forgotten that in India, burdened with her years, problems of social change have been, and continue to be, enormous and complicated. Hoary tradition and social and religious complexes constitute a back-log of history which cannot be easily cleared. And Gandhi was at the same time conservative and revolutionary — he did not, for example, deny the moral validity of the institution of the rich as such, though he sought to change the nature of its working, and ultimately even to eliminate it. His main contribution, thus, was not so much in the sphere of bringing about actual and far-reaching social change as in rousing social consciousness about the necessity of such change. He chose this way perhaps because he was supremely preoccupied with the problem of avoiding violence. It has been suggested in an acute and original study by T.K.N. Unnithan that probably it was not his intention to justify the historical growth of the institution of wealth, for in spite of his concept of "trusteeship" of the rich, he sometimes called methods of accumulation "robbery," but he "ignored it or tolerated it as a result of his conviction that any attempts to question it would result in violence."

It is not to be wondered at that the social policies of the Indian government which swears by Gandhi's name deviate considerably from the Mahatma's ideas. The emphasis, inevitable in today's context, on industrialization, the apparent impossibility of a return to the loosely constructed system of self-sufficient village republics, the renunciation of nonviolence as a guiding principle of State, the lip-service to *sarvodaya* [i.e., the welfare of all] and the inability even to give real shape on a wide scale to an idea so concrete as Basic Education, are examples of this deviation. Throughout his life, Gandhi had been an idealist, in the sense not only that he shrank from philosophical materialism but also that he sought to follow, in all sincerity, certain moral values such as truth and nonviolence and renunciation of sensual pleasures. Throughout his life, he was also ready to be inconsistent, to make certain compromises, to concede, though he did not say it in so many words, that absolute truth and absolute morality are intangibles which cannot be practically pursued; that one like himself, wedded to nonviolence, could sometimes part from it for real-life reasons, as when he went on a recruiting campaign during World War I or during certain phases of World War II agreed to India participating on terms in the war effort. This combination of practicality with the highest idealism made him a most formidable character, and in the period of the struggle for freedom, far and away its most powerful figure. It was this combination, again, which made him useful to the growing bourgeois interests who wanted political power and alongside it a check for mass forces which, properly roused and guided, could follow up freedom with frontal attack on all exploiting elements. To Gandhi himself, all this was probably unclear; he acted as the bent took him, with a hard-headed empiricism which somehow he had adjusted with his basic idealism. This contradiction in himself became clear after the country was free. His disillusionment marked his difference from the Indian bourgeoisie now ensconced in seats of power. While government's post-1947 worries were administrative and the like, Gandhi's agonies were profoundly spiritual. Except as a moral influence, magnificently engaged in healing wounds and repairing casualties of the spirit, Gandhi after independence was sick of soul, weary even of the effort of living, at work no doubt but only because it was the only worship he cared for.

Gandhi's Views on Caste and Untouchability

T. K. N. UNNITHAN

In a wide-ranging study entitled *Gandhi and Free India: A Socio-Economic Study* (1956), T. K. N. Unnithan has employed modern sociological techniques in an attempt to assess the degree and extent of Gandhi's influence on modern Indian society. The brief excerpt which follows discusses the impact of Gandhi's crusade against Untouchability. It should be compared with Dr. Ambedkar's critique of Gandhi's attitudes presented earlier in this volume, and with the references to the subject made in other selections. Dr. Unnithan is a member of the Department of Sociology at the University of Rajasthan.

GANDHI's ideas regarding caste have created much misunderstanding. His defence of the caste system in 1920 gave the impression that he was orthodox in this respect, whereas he held progressive views on other matters. He defended caste as an essential form of social organization. The evils produced by the caste system were no less than those created by the institutions of class. The superiority of the caste system to the class system was that in the former money, in the words of Gandhi "the greatest disruptive force in the world," did not form the basis, whereas distinctions of wealth did form the basis of the class system. Thus to Gandhi the material factor caused the most important difference between class and caste. Caste was to Gandhi an extension of the principle of the family, as both were governed by blood and heredity. He stated that caste was essential for the best possible adjustment of social stability and progress, but he warned that it must not connote superiority or inferiority; it must only recognize different outlooks and corresponding modes of life. But caste as an institution had degenerated to a great extent and the much-feared social stratification on the basis of caste had become the order of the day. Therefore, the practice of caste was not in consonance with its theory. He gradually became more convinced of this and declared, "Down with the monster of caste that masquerades in the guise of *Varna*." Thus he made a distinction between the ideal caste system, as intended by its founders, and the caste system as practiced in India. The former

From T. K. N. Unnithan, *Gandhi and Free India: A Socio-Economic Study* (Groningen, 1956), pp. 68–70, 168–174. By permission of the author.

he called *Varna Dharma* and the latter its distorted practice.

In Gandhi's opinion, it was deviation from the laws of *Varna,* or the principle of caste, that was largely responsible for the economic and spiritual ruin of India. *Varnasrama Dharma* would satisfy the religious, social and economic needs of a community. *Varna,* according to Gandhi's interpretation, meant predetermination of the choice of a man's profession. . . . He saw no reason for anyone to claim superiority. The *Brahmin* had no right to assume superiority; it was against the law of *Varna.* Whereas he accepted the function of a *Brahmin* as "capacity for superior service" he refused to recognize his superiority in status. In the Vedas the four *Varnas* have been compared to the four members of the body, and even if one varna claimed superiority, this had no religious sanction. Gandhi advised social reformers to eradicate this inequality from society. Violation of this law of *Varna* had ended in giving rise to the caste system, with all its horrors, as practised in India. Gandhi regarded caste as a "drag upon Hindu progress" and untouchability as "an excresence upon *Varnasrama.*"

The Untouchables constituted nearly forty million people; they were denied even the ordinary facilities of life. In some parts of India, especially in the South, not only was untouchability practised on a vast scale but unapproachability and invisibility too. Gandhi dedicated his entire life to the service of the *Harijans* (the children of God), the Untouchables. He identified himself with them, calling himself a *Harijan.* He undertook the work of a scavenger and stayed with them in Delhi and Bombay in 1946. In the name of Hinduism and in the name of an independent and prosperous India he appealed to everyone to erase the curse of Untouchability. He addressed meetings from one end of India to the other, denouncing the degeneration it had brought with it. He fasted, fully prepared to sacrifice even his life for the "noble cause of removal of Untouchabil-

ity," or as a penance for the atrocious wrongs committed by his country in the name of religion. . . .

Though from time to time there emerged "stalwart thinkers" and religious leaders like Ramanuja, Chaitanya, Guru Nanak and Vivekananda, who conducted a crusade against oppression, injustice and religious malpractices and advocated revolutionary changes, Hindu society has continued to be static. It is only comparatively recently that it has shown some response to the "challenges of reforms." But even then it took Gandhi almost a quarter of a century to secure the right of Harijans to enter temples where only caste Hindus could worship. However, signs of the system's crumbling from within offer some hope.

In the background of this slow change in the system, we find the monumental work of Mahatma Gandhi. Apart from him the lifelong services of several others like Amritlal Thakkar or Jawaharlal Nehru have also made a great contribution. Ambedkar has rendered considerable service to the cause of the Untouchables. Perhaps his contributions would have been more effective if he had worked along with Gandhi instead of taking an independent attitude. Gandhi's work, which set the change in motion, is being continued on the same lines by the *Harijan Sevak Sangh* (an organization founded by Gandhi himself for the exclusive service of the depressed castes) and *Gandhi Smarak Nidhi* (Gandhi Memorial Fund, which is being utilized for the furtherance of Gandhian ideals). Besides these, there are several private societies and social service organizations at work. The Rama Krishna Mission, a number of Christian missionaries and the Depressed Classes Associations are also forces working in favour of change.

Influenced mainly by Mahatma Gandhi, the Congress had accepted the removal of untouchability as a primary and necessary means for the goal of social equality in independent India. Therefore, when they came to power in 1947, they were obliged to execute their pledge. . . . Article 17 of the constitution relating to Fundamental Rights declares:

Untouchability is abolished and its practice in any form forbidden. The enforcement of any disability arising out of untouchability shall be an offence punishable in accordance with law. . . .

The persistence of the caste system and the practice of untouchability is a problem for the Government to tackle. But the situation is accentuated by the overt resistance offered by orthodox and illiterate groups who attribute the evil to the existence of Destiny and who want to maintain the present social stratification intact. . . .

The practice of untouchability and its parent, the caste system, continue to exist. The social system is so deeply imbedded in the Indian mind that legislative measures alone are of no great consequence. Even after the enforcement of the recent [Untouchability Offences] Act [of 1955], there have been fresh revivals of the practice of untouchability and of the severe resistance to any form of social change. . . .

Although we thus find resistances to reform measures adopted by the government, we cannot ignore the fact that there have been *some* changes in the practice of caste regulations or untouchability, even if we make allowances for changes which would have occurred anyhow. Resistances are natural when means are devised for altering the course of life of an orthodox community, and in some ways visibility of resistances to reform measures serves as an indication of the contributions of the measures already adopted and of the necessity of further reforms for the desired changes.

Of the reasons for these slow changes the Gandhian contribution — the contributions Gandhi himself made directly and those caused through the influence of his ideas on the government and the people — looms as the most prominent. . . .

Yet it can hardly be said that caste and Untouchability do not constitute a serious problem in India at present.

In our opinion Untouchability cannot be easily eradicated from India by palliative measures undertaken from time to time. For the permanent removal of this age-old evil, its root, namely, the caste system, has first to be broken. Gandhi's contribution would have been far greater had he directed his opposition simultaneously against the caste system which has given sanction to untouchability than to the latter alone.

Gandhi and the Hindu-Muslim Problem

INDIRA ROTHERMUND

It has been difficult for students of Indian nationalism to see the rivalries of the Indian National Congress and the Muslim League — or of Gandhi and Jinnah — as part of an integral whole. Typically, the sympathies of writers have led them to emphasize either the role of the Congress or of the League, and to consider the other body only as a disruptive element. The merit of Indira Rothermund's treatment of the subject in her study, *The Philosophy of Restraint: Mahatma Gandhi's Strategy and Indian Politics* (1963) lies in the way she analyzes the interacting nature of the two developments.

THE developments that led to the partition of India . . . are intimately connected with the aims and policies of the Indian National Congress and they determine at the present day the tensions which have jeopardized India's message to the world. At the root of these tensions are the principles of national unity and communal integrity, two principles which became more and more opposed to each other as national independence drew nearer. The exponents of these two principles were Gandhi and Jinnah. As the one advanced towards national unity, the other insisted more and more upon communal integrity. The progress of the one was a challenge to the other. Before Gandhi asserted his leadership in India Jinnah had been an ambassador of Hindu-Muslim unity. And, as one may say, being displaced from his position in Indian politics Jinnah was compelled "to carve out a new empire."

The national tragedy which was a consequence of this situation has five acts and almost resembles a classical tragedy. Act One: The Lucknow Pact between the Congress and the Muslim League which accepted separate electorates for Hindus and Muslims. Act Two: The *Khilafat* movement. Act Three: The Muslim League versus the Congress and the Pakistan plan. Act Four: The partition of India. Act Five: The death of Gandhi.

As in a true tragedy, the heroes collaborate with the forces of fate to prepare the disaster. The best actions serve as steps toward the tragic end. The protagonists participate in the tragic pursuit as interdependent partners; and from the raising of the curtain the tragic relations are set.

Let us examine the acts of the tragedy more closely. The first act begins when Mohammed Ali Jinnah, a moderate politician and a member of the Congress, becomes in addition a member of the Muslim League. The act leads up to the Lucknow Pact of 1916 in which Jinnah serves as the spokesman of the Muslim League and reaches an agreement with Tilak, the Hindu leader, under which separate electorates for Hindus and Muslims are accepted. The Pact furthermore implies . . . a plan of federated agitation in which Jinnah is the recognized leader of the Indian Muslims. With this recognition Jinnah has become fixed in a communal role and from that time on he would insist on his position as the spokesman for his community and would be ready to collaborate

From Indira Rothermund, *The Philosophy of Restraint: Mahatma Gandhi's Strategy and Indian Politics* (Bombay, 1963), pp. 98–102, 109–111, 113–115. By permission of Popular Prakashan, Bombay.

with any authentic Hindu leader who is willing to accept a parallel communal role.

However, towards the end of the act Gandhi appears on the scene. He does not conceive of himself as a communal leader but as a national leader, and will put up a lifelong struggle against communalism and for national unity.

The second act shows Gandhi as a national leader of Muslims and Hindus. Under his leadership the Khilafat movement, a demonstration against Britain's policy towards the Caliph in Turkey, becomes a national issue in which communal differences are forgotten. Jinnah observes this development with alarm and is concerned about Gandhi's agitation of the masses. As a Moderate and constitutional agitator, Jinnah is opposed to an appeal to the masses. He resigns his Congress membership. The Khilafat Committee replaces the Muslim League and Jinnah becomes more and more isolated. However, with the revolution in Turkey the Khilafat issue is deflated and the tide turns.

The third act brings the turning point. Gandhi's fast for Hindu-Muslim unity in 1924 has no definite results. The Khilafat Muslims become gradually alienated from Gandhi. On the other hand Jinnah, who still tries to mediate between conservative and moderate Muslims on the one side and the Congress on the other, fails in a number of these attempts and has to draw closer to the conservative Muslims. Gandhi's second civil disobedience campaign, which begins in 1930, widens the rift, and while Gandhi breaks the Salt Law, Jinnah participates in the first Round Table Conference in London. In the same year the poet Iqbal announced for the first time a Pakistan plan at a Muslim League conference. Jinnah spurns this idea at first, but when the Congress wins the first election in 1937 with an overwhelming majority and refuses to share power with the Muslim League, all old apprehensions combine and Jinnah becomes its spokesman. Pakistan becomes his watchword, and he tries to reach the Muslim masses in an attempt to emulate Gandhi's hold on the Indian masses and the surprising success of Congress Muslims among Muslim voters. Against Gandhi's quest for national unity, which is intended to overcome communalism, he hurls his slogan of the "two nations." Jinnah, who wanted to collaborate if assured of his position, is now for separation because his position has not been recognized by Gandhi. Astonishment has become disillusionment and disillusion has finally become hatred. Jinnah, the cool, rational and arrogant lawyer, becomes a fervent and fanatic leader of the masses.

The fourth act brings the consummation of Jinnah's plan, the partition of India. His concept of the "two nations" wins a bloody victory over Gandhi's concept of the communal and national unity of India. (It is almost as if the man who once warned Gandhi of the masses had now unleashed them in order to demonstrate his point.) The "two nations" concept has been strong enough to release forces of apprehension, while Gandhi's concept of Hindu-Muslim unity had not been solid enough to give a basis to universal cooperation. Jinnah knew about the apprehensions of the Indian Muslims because they were his own apprehensions; Gandhi had neglected to take these apprehensions into account. It was difficult for him to become aware of them, because his Muslim associates like Abdul Ghaffar Khan were self-reliant people who knew no apprehensions.

The fifth act: During the terrors of partition Gandhi begins to doubt his achievements. He walks alone. Finally he tries to avert whatever he can of the consequences of the disaster. His last great action — the fast for Hindu-Muslim peace in Delhi in 1948 — was, like his first great national campaign, the Khilafat campaign of 1920, dedicated to Hindu-Muslim unity. Soon after this fast he is shot by a Hindu radical because he stood for Hindu-Muslim unity.

The question of fault, as in any tragedy, is largely beyond the protagonists; and although Gandhi made the pronouncement that "Pakistan is sin," he would hardly have referred to Jinnah as a sinner pure and simple. The apprehensions which Jinnah represented and which he heightened were nevertheless not of his own creation. Indeed it might be said that Jinnah himself had tried to escape these apprehensions during his long career as a politician. But they caught up with him when he saw those Muslims whom he represented defeated in his own realm, the constitutional and parliamentary field, in the election of 1937. From then on he decided to turn these apprehensions to profit in rallying the Muslims around the banner of the Muslim League.

What were these apprehensions? They were the fears of the Indian Muslims that as democratic processes were introduced in India, the Hindus would overwhelm the Muslims because of their majority in representative institutions. The lack of a sufficiently numerous Muslim middle class which could assert its influence in such institutions, heightened these fears. . . .

Could Gandhi have stopped the rising tide of communalism? Could he have accommodated Jinnah in one way or the other? Did he miss opportunities to bridge the gap between Hindus and Muslims? And is it true, as a Muslim writer says: "Not Jinnah but Gandhi will the future generations hold responsible for the decision of Pakistan?"

In these matters Gandhi's strength became his weakness, because his implicit belief in national unity and his compassionate contact with the masses made him overlook the importance of politicians who posed as representatives of this or that group, and his dedicated struggle for independence and social reconstruction, started at the village level, made him extremely indifferent to federal or central constitutions and other legal constructions.

For these reasons Jinnah the politician and constitutionalist and Gandhi the reformer and popular leader had to operate on completely different planes and could never come to any real understanding. If Gandhi had succeeded in his attempts to strike at the root of Muslim communalism and to secure a lasting Hindu-Muslim cooperation, this difference between Jinnah and Gandhi would have been of no importance, and in such circumstances Jinnah would have long since been forgotten. But Gandhi did not succeed in these attempts (again it was his strength which became his weakness); his appreciation of the fundamental truths of the Koran and his reliance upon his Muslim friends made him overlook the social and historical conditions of the Muslims of his time. The first serious consequence of this fact was his participation in the *Khilafat* movement. It was a curious reversal of the constellation: In 1916 Jinnah the Moderate Muslim had made the Lucknow Pact with Tilak the Hindu Extremist; in 1920 Gandhi the Moderate Hindu led a movement of conservative Muslims. Both constellations were short-lived, for Tilak died four years after the Lucknow Pact and with him died the spirit of this Pact, and the *Khilafat* was dissolved by Kemal Pasha four years after Gandhi had espoused the *Khilafat* cause. After this round of events any large-scale, top-level organization of Hindu-Muslim unity was never again attempted. Gandhi relied upon village-level Hindu-Muslim unity; this village-level unity, however, in order to imply nationwide unity, would have demanded an Islamic reform similar to Gandhi's reform of Hinduism. Gandhi, not being a Muslim, could not perform the task of reforming Islam from within.

In order to understand the full significance of this fact we must turn our attention to Islam as a religion and as a historical force. . . .

Most modern reform movements in Islam have not been founded on the mystical, tolerant, universalist Sufism,[1] but rather on a puritan, fundamentalist approach to Islam as a reaction against Sufism. While the Sufis had stressed the salvation of the

[1] A trend in Islamic thought and practice emphasizing devotion rather than ritual, personal religious experience rather than formal theology. [Editor's note]

individual soul and its union with God, the fundamentalists reemphasized the corporate character of the brotherhood of believers.

This corporate character of religious reform movements has had an influence on secular movements among Muslims; furthermore it was reinforced by the common lack of secular advancement among Muslims, which had led to common apprehensions. . . .

The Congress thought in terms of national unity and wanted to identify itself with all Indian communities; the Muslim League, however, envisioned a corporate "side by side" of Hindus and Muslims and wanted therefore to "incorporate" all Muslims within itself and to regard the Congress as a parallel Hindu corporation. The insistence of the Congress on identifying itself with Muslims and its refusal to be a Hindu corporation was deeply resented by the Muslim League. The two approaches to Hindu-Muslim Unity — the method of incorporation and pact on the one side and the method of identification on the other — were incompatible. Consequently the Muslim League thought that the Congress was hypocritical, intransigent and cunning, and the Congress thought that the Muslim League was presumptuous, separatist and unpatriotic.

Not all Indian Muslims found their political creed in this corporate ideology, and many of them found their way into the Congress. The most prominent of these Congress Muslims had a Sufi background like that of Maulana Abul Kalam Azad; their philosophy had more in common with Gandhi's thought. It was therefore very difficult for Gandhi to understand the corporate claim of the Muslim League. In addition, any understanding with the Muslim League was barred to Gandhi, since it would have involved a disowning of his own Muslim associates, whom the Muslim League regarded as traitors to the Muslim cause.

In his assuredness that India "was with him" against partition, Gandhi overlooked the fact that many politicians were not with him. These politicians looked first of all at the constitutional alternatives and could not find any common ground in that field. The standard battle between centralists and federalists, which had been fought so many times in history, was fought in India with the added vigor of communal apprehension on one side, and on the other the awareness of the need for a strong central government which could preserve a free and unified India. Gandhi's indifference to these questions gave rise to two things: a strong, unified Republic of India with a stable, centralized and popular government on the one hand, and the partition of India on the other. His victory was bound up with his defeat.

Gandhian Ideology and
the Indian National Congress

PITAMBAR DATT KAUSHIK

Whether they approved or disapproved of Gandhi's leadership, most of the authors of the preceding selections stressed the degree to which that leadership was decisive in shaping the course which was taken by the Indian National Congress. In the reading which follows, P. D. Kaushik, a political scientist at Saugar University, takes a different approach by examining the differences between Gandhi's ideas and outlook and those of other influential leaders of the Congress.

NOBODY can dispute that the Congress ideology after the First World War was mainly a creation of Gandhi, yet, it is too much to say that the Congress was a "one-man show" or that the Congress ideology was identical with the Gandhian principles. On the contrary there were significant differences between the two and more than once Gandhi suffered defeat in Congress parleys. In 1924, this so-called dictator wept openly in a meeting of the A.I.C.C. [All-India Congress Committee] because 70 out of 148 members who voted believed in political murders — a clear indication of the fact their nonviolence was only skin deep. In 1934, he retired from the Congress in sheer disgust. In 1939, Subhas Chandra Bose was elected to the Congress Presidency in spite of his open and determined opposition. In June, 1940, the Working Committee bluntly turned down his request to extend the principle of nonviolence to war and in December 1941 even formally relieved him of the leadership of the Congress. . . .

Though Gandhian thought was the main source of Congress Ideology, yet there were also other thought currents which pro-foundly influenced its development. These thought currents were represented by C. R. Das and Motilal Nehru before 1927 and by Jawaharlal Nehru and Subhas Chandra Bose after 1927. . . .

Both Das and Motilal believed in swift action. They had no patience with slow-moving devices like Gandhi's constructive program. They could enthusiastically take up non-cooperation or civil disobedience because there was swift and breathless activity in them, but when non-cooperation was suspended their way lay not in constructive program but in council entry, where they could beard the British lion in his den. . . .

The difference between the ideology and outlook of Gandhi on the one hand and Das and Motilal on the other was best illustrated in their respective attitudes towards nonviolence and non-cooperation. Both Das and Motilal used to swear by nonviolence and non-cooperation. As early as 1919 Motilal spoke of his faith in "truth, fearlessness and nonviolence." And in 1922 Das claimed to be ". . . one of those who hold to nonviolence on principles." But their nonviolence was very dif-

From Pitambar Datt Kaushik, "Non-Gandhian Influences on Pre-Independence Ideology of Indian National Congress," *The Modern Review* (Calcutta), October, 1962, pp. 274–279. By permission of the author.

ferent from its Gandhian prototype. It had little place for the doctrines of "change of heart of the enemy" or "non-embarrassment of the enemy." The nonviolence of Das had room even for political murders and when on June 27th, 1924, Gandhi moved the resolution condemning the murder of Mr. Earnest Day by Gopi Nath Saha, Das hotly opposed it. To Das and Nehru nonviolence was not a high moral principle connoting a search of truth through the method of love but only absence of direct violence. . . .

Next to Gandhi, Jawaharlal Nehru was the greatest architect of the ideology and program of the 20th century Congress. He came to prominence in Congress after 1925 with his slogan of "Complete Independence," and compelled Gandhi and others to make it the creed of the Congress at Lahore in 1929. From the very beginning he became the leader of the left wing of the Congress. . . . Although he . . . was reconciled with Gandhi to an extent that Gandhi declared that "Jawaharlal will be my successor," yet there continued to be many important differences between the two.

The basic difference between the two was that while Gandhi represented the "religious mind" of India, Nehru was the embodiment of her "secular instinct." Gandhi regarded politics and religions as inseparable; Nehru believed that "usually religion becomes an asocial quest for God or the Absolute, and the religious man is concerned far more with his own salvation than with the good of society." Under Gandhi's influence he was more and more "attracted" towards the doctrine of nonviolence, but he "did not give an absolute allegiance to it." He recognized the necessity of force. "Everything that comes in the way," he said, "will have to be removed, gently if possible, forcibly if necessary. And there seems little doubt that coercion will often be necessary." While Gandhi wanted to make Congress an instrument of the spiritual regeneration of India, Nehru wished to make it the spear-

head of economic and social revolution. Nehru believed that "without a conscious ideology and objective the energy and enthusiasm of the masses must end largely in smoke" and hence wanted a clear picture of independent India and *swaraj* for which the Congress was fighting. But Gandhi regarded these questions as premature. To him the real thing was the creation of the true religious and moral spirit among the people and the development of a sound national character. Gandhi had little faith in foreign propaganda and believed that the world was bound to recognize India's claims as soon as the nation developed an overwhelming strength from within. But Nehru was an internationalist and believed that the "Indian problem is not only a national problem." ". . . if we ignore the world," he warned his countrymen, "we do so at our own peril" because "India today is a part of a world movement. Not only China, Turkey, Persia and Egypt, but also Russia and the countries of the West are taking part in this movement, and India cannot isolate herself from it."

It was, however, in the field of economic ideology that the differences between Gandhi and Nehru were most marked. "Few of us, I think," wrote Nehru, "accepted Gandhiji's old ideas about machinery and modern civilization. . . ." Gandhi denounced industrialization as "a curse for mankind" and wanted "every village of India" to be a self-supporting and self-contained unit, exchanging only such necessary commodities with other villages where they are not locally produceable. He had little faith in state planning and kept himself aloof from the National Planning Committee organized by the Congress in 1938. On the contrary, Nehru had great faith in Planning and stood for "the rapid industrialization of the country." Gandhi repudiated the theory of class struggle, ruled out the abolition of private property and advanced his famous doctrine of "Trusteeship" as the solution of economic problems. Nehru, on the other hand, was "convinced that the only key to the solution of world problems and of India's problems lies in socialism," which meant ". . . the ending of vested interest in land and industry, as well as the feudal and autocratic Indian state system, . . . ending of private property . . . and the replacement of the present profit system by a higher ideal of co-operation." Both Gandhi and Nehru aimed at the amelioration of the peasantry but while Gandhi's program for achieving this end was a program of spinning wheel and village industries, of *Swadeshi* and *satyagraha,* of Trusteeship and change of heart on the part of *zamindars,* Nehru's program was a program of rent reduction, debt cancellation and abolition of landlordism. . . .

Yet one must not overemphasize these differences, because when all is said and done it remains true that to a large extent Nehru was "the Plato to Gandhi's Socrates" and having put his "faith in him (Gandhi) gave him almost a blank cheque." He never questioned the Gandhian leadership but tried to mould the Congress ideology in accordance with his ideas within the four corners of that leadership. In that he succeeded admirably and gave an orientation to it which it could never have had under pure Gandhism. Briefly speaking, he introduced the Independence creed, when Gandhi was flirting with the idea of Dominion Status; created interest in world problems and laid the foundations of the future foreign policy of independent India; brought socialism into the Congress; gave a concrete shape to the concept of national Planning and saved the Congress from falling into the labyrinth of unadulterated pacifism.

Another person who influenced the Congress ideology profoundly, though not to an extent commensurate with Gandhi or even with Nehru, was Subhas Chandra Bose. In the beginning Subhas and Jawahar jointly led the revolt against Gandhi. At that time, except that Subhas disliked Communism while Jawahar admired Russia, their respective ideologies were the same. But it could not last long. Nehru's ever-growing loyalty to Gandhi sealed the fate of their friendship. . . . One became the political heir apparent of Gandhi, the other the standard bearer of revolt against Gandhian leadership.

Strange as it seems, Bose was as much a man of religion as Gandhi was, yet, for him religion had no place in politics. Instead he believed that "A subject race has nothing but politics," and his *mantra* [credo] was: "Consecration of our life at the altar of freedom." He had little faith in nonviolence and none in the doctrine of purity of means. In his opinion, "Gandhism had been found wanting, because it was wedded to nonviolence. . . ." Gandhi's spiritualism had no attractions for Bose. ". . . ascetics and yogis," he said, "have held . . . honoured place in society, but it is not their lead that we shall want to follow if we are to create a new India, at once free, happy and great. . . . We have to live in the present." . . . Gandhi was always ready to negotiate with the enemy, but Bose advocated a path of "uncompromising militancy." . . .

On economic issues also Bose and Gandhi differed radically. Bose deplored the Gandhian school of thought for creating "a feeling and an impression that modernism is bad, large-scale production is an evil, wants should not be increased and standard of living should not be raised . . . and that the soul is so important that physical culture and military training can be ignored." He considered Gandhi's program to be "bourgeois," and wanted the Congress to "adopt a radical economic programme" "including abolition of land-lordism . . . extension of the cooperative movement . . . a comprehensive scheme of industrial development under state ownership and state control."

The differences between Gandhi and Bose are best reflected in the symbols they adopted. The Congress under Gandhi as well as the Indian National Army under Bose adopted as their standard a tricolor in green, white and saffron, but while Gandhi placed a spinning wheel in its center, Bose replaced the wheel by a spring-ing tiger. . . .

A man with such ideas and such ability as Bose possessed was bound to come into conflict with Gandhi. He had, in fact, in 1939, humbled Gandhi in the first round of the struggle, but was ultimately defeated and expelled from the Congress. But Gandhi could expel from the Congress only Bose the person; he was unable to expel his ideas. For a long time to come the ideas and ideals of Bose remained the beacon of a substantial number of Congressmen.

Besides Nehru and Bose other elements which provided non-Gandhian thought currents in the Congress were the Socialists led by Acharya Narendra Deo and Jai Prakash Narayan; the Communists led by Masani and Asaf Ali; the *Kisan Sabhaites* [Peasant Leaguers] led by Swami Sahajanand Saraswati. . . .

The cumulative effect of all these influences was that official Congress ideology and program parted company from Gandhian principles at many points.

Firstly, nonviolence could never become a creed with the Congress, but always remained a policy. Not once but twice — at Lahore Congress in 1929, and at Bombay Congress in 1934 — Gandhi tried to secure the change of "peaceful and legitimate means" into "truthful and nonviolent means" but both the times, he had to pocket his pride. . . .

Secondly, they differed in their attitude towards non-cooperation. Gandhi was a non-cooperator by conviction. He regarded "non-cooperation with an unjust Government . . . a duty." But to the Congress non-cooperation was not a "duty" but an "instrument" to be used for achieving the country's independence. That is why as soon as Gandhi suspended the non-cooperation movement in 1922, the Congress rapidly moved towards the policy of council-entry and responsive cooperation, though Gandhi was hotly opposed to it.

Thirdly, the Congress did not give complete allegiance to the doctrine of the Purity of Means. As Pattabhi Sitaramayya remarked,

With him (Gandhi) what counts is direction, not destination, attempt not attainment, means not ends.

With the Congress it was almost the reverse. What counted with the Congress was destination rather than the direction, attainment rather than the attempt, ends rather than the means. This is why when after the outbreak of the Second World War there seemed a possibility of attaining independence on the basis of active participation in the war effort, the Congress threw overboard Gandhi as well as his nonviolence.

Fourthly, it gave a very very qualified allegiance to Gandhi's economic views. It was not very enthusiastic about Gandhi's constructive program. It "has . . . always been in favor of the industrialization of India. . . ." The Congressmen in general never accepted Gandhi's views about machinery and modern civilization. The "music of the spinning wheel" was only faintly audible to them and they had only a skin-deep faith in the ethics or the economics of *khaddar*. Gandhi's attempts to introduce "Yarn Franchise" in the Congress organization ended in dismal failure.

Last, but not the least, the Congress refused to become "primarily an instrument of moral and spiritual regeneration of India" and confined its activities mainly to the political and socio-economic fields. That is why when during the Second World War, Gandhi urged the Congress to offer unconditional moral cooperation to Britain, the Congress not only refused to oblige, but also absolved him of its leadership. Soon, of course, the Congress had to request Gandhi again "to take the lead and guide the nation," but the aftermath of the "Quit India" resolution proved almost "a parting of ways." Till June 1945 because of the incarceration of most of the important Congress leaders, there was little activity on the part of the Congress, save the revolution of 1942–43, which was far from being nonviolent in the Gandhian sense of the term. After June, 1945, events moved fast and on August 15, 1947, India saw the dawn of independence. The attainment of independence, however, further widened the gulf between Gandhi and the Congress. Prior to independence the Congress leaders had to accept many of the Gandhian tenets because they were unable to put forward either an alternative plan of action or an alternative leadership. But in the post-independence era they rejected or sidetracked many of the Gandhian ideals and ideas as too lofty, medieval or impractical.

But it does not mean that the Congress has completely renounced Gandhi or that its loyalty to Gandhi was only a make-believe. The fact is that like other great prophets — Buddha, Christ or Mohammad — Gandhi also was too great, his ideals too high to be completely followed by his disciples. Naturally they often seem to drift away from their masters. But the master's teachings always remained as an inspiring ideal which is never achieved but whose imprint always remains ineffaceable. Prior to independence, barring some notable exceptions, the Congress followed the lead of the Mahatma. Since then it might have drifted further away from Gandhi but the stamp of the master is still there and perhaps will never be completely erased away.

TWO SUMMARY STATEMENTS

An American View of Gandhi

W. NORMAN BROWN

There are few Americans who are better qualified to interpret Indian developments than W. Norman Brown (1892–   ), Professor of Sanskrit and
Chairman of the Department of South Asia Regional Studies at the University
of Pennsylvania. In the following selection, from his *The United States and
India and Pakistan* (1953), he applies his wide understanding of traditional
Indian civilization and his equally perceptive analysis of modern Indian history
to the task of interpreting Gandhi's role.

INDIA today considers Gandhi the author of her independence. He had her
confidence more than any other of her
leaders; he organized the resistance to the
imperialist government; he swayed to his
will politicians who had no belief in his
mystical theories; he is the master whom
all public figures profess to follow. His
saintly life won for him the courtesy title
of *Mahatma*, "the Great-Souled," and his
warmth, humor, kindliness, and wisdom
gained him the devotion of India's masses
as their personal refuge. This they acknowledged by another title *Bapu* or
Bapuji, "Father," which was affectionately
applied during his lifetime and after his
death was used by the government of India
on a commemorative stamp. The night he
died Jawaharlal Nehru in a moving broad-
cast said, ". . . the light has gone out of
our lives and there is darkness everywhere."
His death rites were celebrated in every
corner of India and wherever Indians lived
abroad. His ashes were minutely divided
and sent to all parts of the country to be
scattered in the rivers and lakes and so to
be mingled with that sacred water by

which the whole land lives. No man in
these times, if ever, has commanded so
much affection in India, nor has anyone's
death been so deeply grieved. He was to
his countrymen patriot and prophet in one;
after he died it was a fear of his closest associates that he might be translated into a
deity. . . .

Gandhi was first of all a religious genius,
and his basic objectives were morally ori-
ented. When he led the struggle for self-
rule (*swaraj*) and later preached universal
uplift (*sarvodaya*) as the social ideal, and
land gift (*bhudan, bhoodan*) by the rich
to the landless, he did so that India might
achieve her moral destiny. Every kind of
human activity, social, political, commer-
cial, or other, he felt should spring from a
religious motive, no sanctions were ultimately valid except those of religion. The
religion he professed was undeviatingly
Hinduism, yet that type of Hinduism
which tolerates all shades of opinion in
others. . . . There was much in his personal belief that had parallels in western
creeds along with much that had not, as
when with his monotheism, faith in mys-

Reprinted by permission of the publishers from W. Norman Brown, *The United States and India and
Pakistan*, revised and enlarged edition, pp. 89, 92–93, 307–308, 94–104. Cambridge, Mass.: Harvard
University Press, Copyright, 1953 and 1963, by the President and Fellows of Harvard College.

tical realization of God, belief in the moral and spiritual value of physical suffering, and reliance upon the human will, he clung staunchly to the doctrines of rebirth, of *karma* that gives scope to the human will and thus determines the conditions of rebirth, of caste that allots a man his proper status in life, of protection for the sacred cow, that "poem of pity," wherein man recognizes his eternal kinship with the animal creation.

His great strength in religion lay on the practical side, in applied ethics, the principles of conduct which he advocated and the means of fulfilling them. There, too, he was profoundly Hindu and humanitarian. The vows of those who came to live in his retreat, always known as an *ashram,* included truthfulness; *ahinsa,* that is, noninjury of living creatures, whether by word, deed, or thought; the practice of labor; celibacy; restraint of the desire for savory food; nonthieving, carried to the extreme of not owning more than one can use; patronage of one's native industries to the exclusion of foreign; fearlessness; amelioration of the lot of the Untouchables; the use of native Indian languages for education; the weaving of homespun cloth. These practices were to cleanse and enlarge the lives of those observing them and to be a guide to other Indians. Their combined purpose was to work the regeneration of India, a return to a golden, if mythical past.

In the application of these principles he long labored with an unswerving intensity and he contributed much to India's social improvement. The campaign he waged against untouchability, which reached its climax in his "fast unto death," September 1932, was the most spectacular of the many efforts made by Indians in that direction and should be regarded as the most influential force in producing in India's present constitution the clause which says "untouchability is abolished." He was deeply concerned with the conditions of India's peasantry. Cottage spinning and weaving, advocated by him, have, where tried, at

times been mildly helpful in temporarily alleviating rural economic misery. He taught a "new system of education" (*nai talim*) for India in which learning was coupled with the practice of a trade, and this had some practical advantage to his country. He was not, it happened, very sophisticated in respect of exploitation of labor in modern industry, but took an ideal mid-Victorian attitude on relations of employer and employees.

*   *   *

When Congress launched its first non-cooperation campaign (1920–1922), Gandhi, who was deeply concerned by peasant problems, won over the existing peasant organizations. It was a kind of paradox for him to do so, for Congress was getting its financial support and administrative direction from the middle classes, who were likely to be landowners. At that time Congress had no constructive policy on either agrarian or industrial labor problems. Gandhi's own attitude was that no one class should benefit at the expense of another but all should unselfishly work together. Landlords and industrialists, peasants and workers should not treat each other as enemies but should practice mutual forbearance and tolerance. The one should not withhold rent or go on strikes; the other should provide good living and working conditions, take only a just amount in rent, and pay fair wages. Under the application of this teaching the landlords lost nothing and the peasants gained nothing.

*   *   *

The underlying basis of Gandhi's social and political program was simple. "My uniform experience," he says in his autobiography, "has convinced me that there is no other God than Truth. And if every page of these chapters does not proclaim that the only means for the realization of Truth is Ahinsa, I shall deem all my pains in writing these chapters to have been in vain." And again, "To see the universal and all-pervading Spirit of Truth face to face one must be able to love the meanest of creatures as oneself. And a man who aspires after that cannot afford to keep out of any field of life. That is why my devotion to truth has drawn me into the field of politics; and I can say without the slightest hesitation and yet in all humility that those who say that religion has nothing to do with politics do not know what religion means."

The application of these principles was as follows. India, and for that matter the world at large, was in bondage to evil as the result of departure from the pure teachings of religion. In India the disease, he said, showed itself in many symptoms, of which subservience to a foreign power was only one; others of major importance were the Hindu-Muslim antipathy, the social crime of untouchability, the poverty of the masses. The cure was to be spiritual regeneration, religious reform, and, if this were accomplished, all the unhappy features of modern Indian life would automatically vanish. What remained, then, was to determine what things were false and what were true, and it was here that "nonviolence," that is, noninjury of other creatures, came into association with truth. . . .

It was the preoccupation with *ahinsa* that was primarily responsible for Indians' esteem for Gandhi. It was not so much his acceptance of bare poverty, weighty as that was — others who had done so had not the same popularity; and one who had not accepted such poverty, Jawaharlal Nehru, was second only to him in the affections of India. Neither was it his individual political, social, and economic views, with which large numbers of his ardent admirers were in greater or lesser disagreement. Nor was it finally the mere fact that he was sincerely devoted to religion, for so were many other Indians. But it was his precise interpretation of the essence of religion that won response from his fellow countrymen, and the fact that he provided a channel for action in keeping with traditional Hindu ideals. The Hindu really believes in the doctrine of *ahinsa*, though through poverty, custom, lack of imagination, or mere human frailty he may often fail to practice it, and in making an idol of Mahatma Gandhi he revealed his own deepest self.

*   *   *

That India trusted Gandhi was due, next to his promulgation of *ahinsa*, to the completeness of his ascetic and religious life. If nothing else would have gripped the imagination of Indians, his fasts and his hunger strikes would, being ancient and honored Indian practices. Similarly the habit of silence, which he observed every Monday, is true to the equally ancient Hindu notion that a sage seeking truth can find it only through concentrated silent meditation: a common Sanskrit word for "silence" is *mauna,* which means literally "quality of an ascetic" (*muni*). At the same time Gandhi did not strain the intellect of the masses with ideas that were difficult to comprehend or were revolutionary of the Hindu tradition. He accepted the old dogmas in principle; he wanted only to modify them in application. The terms designating them were symbols for the old forms of the ideas, which the people at large felt to be valid, and also for the new forms, which he gave them, and thus the folk and he had a measure of mutual understanding. And lacking the freedom of the artist that so often arouses distrust in the general public, he had the self-confident strength of the puritan. He spoke to the people simply, forcefully, and on issues of prime importance, while his sincerity was coupled with a personal charm that made his propagandizing a work of genius.

So much freedom from conservatism and traditional prejudice was offensive to strict orthodox upper-caste Hinduism. Throughout his career Gandhi was subject to denunciation from such elements. At various times and in different parts of India he was met on his travels with open hostility and sometimes violence from those who disapproved of him. It was one such person, belonging to disaffected orthodoxy, who finally assassinated him.

Possibly the greatest contribution which Gandhi gave to nationalism, greater even than his convincing justification of its aims, was a philosophy of resistance on which he developed a practical technique of revolution. This was his political mass use of nonviolence. Though this abstract principle had an ancient and honorable tradition in India, it had never before been applied there on a concrete national scale to achieve a broad political end. He persuaded Congress to adopt it, in spite of misgivings and disbelief among many Congressmen. To see how it operated we may look at a simple, uncomplicated average case of a sort that attracted no special notice in the press when it occurred but shows nonviolent resistance in typical application.

At Jubbulpore (Jabalpur) early in January 1932, Congress sympathizers attempted a parade and, when ordered by police to disperse, merely halted, squatted on the roadway, filling it from edge to edge, and refused to move. The police charged and beat them with *lathis*, which are wooden staves, six to eight feet in length, shod at one end with metal. The demonstrators offered no resistance, but submitted to the beating without retaliation, and, still without offering violence, let themselves be bundled off by the hundreds to jail. In 1920–1922 and again in 1930–1932 scenes of this sort were common all over India. Often a demonstration would be preceded by a closing of shops for a one or more days' cessation of business (*hartal*). Arrests were inevitable and so numerous that the government had to set up many special detention camps and confinement quarters to care for the prisoners. It was a form of conflict that left the victorious government embarrassed and shamefaced. Though nonviolent resistance seemed to fail in each single case, in the end it produced an atmosphere in which the government appeared to act illogically, inhumanly, indefensibly.

Gandhi's method differed from any used by his nationalist predecessors. Some of these had proceeded secularly and opportunistically, with no consciously rationalized philosophy of resistance, merely employing argument and debate. Most early Congressmen were of this sort. They were for change through constitutional means, by "evolution rather than revolution," and their method was to use persuasion upon the British in the hope that well-reasoned claims would meet with success. This was the method of Gokhale; it was still the method used by the Indian Moderates or Liberals, such as Sir Tej Bahadur Sapru, Mr. Srinivasa Sastri, and Dr. Mukund Ramrao Jayakar, as recently as 1945. It never got effective response from the British. Such men had the respect of thoughtful Indians for their patriotism, honesty, and political sagacity, but the masses rarely if ever heard of them, acquired no confidence in their method, and never gave them popular support.

Some others of Gandhi's predecessors invoked a religious sanction, but not that of religion in its compassionate, nonviolent mood. Rather, it was that of religion when it uncompromisingly strikes down an opponent with physical force. The most noteworthy of these was B. G. Tilak. The god of Tilak and his school was no more shocked by violence than was Jesus, when he said "I came not to send peace, but a sword." The precise means of attacking the infidel foreigner they borrowed from Russian terrorists, who adopted the pistol and the bomb, and the bomb was greeted by Tilak as an "amulet" for India. There followed a long list of political murders and attempted murders in eastern, western, and northern India down to the time of Gandhi's assassination in January 1948. With this violence became associated, especially in Bengal, worship of the Mother Goddess, under the locally popular form of Kali, who is to be appeased by blood, and the victims of assassination were her sacrifices. The Mother Goddess is perhaps the oldest of all existing cults in India, being known to us from the Harappa culture in the third millennium B.C., and in her service young political radicals often showed a marked degree of physical courage and selfless religious devotion.

Political murder also added unto itself robbery with the purpose of securing funds for prosecuting nationalist aims. Such terrorism gave the government its chief grounds for refusing to negotiate with the nationalists. Though the Indian National Congress as a whole did not endorse this violence, many of its members were sympathetic and condoned it. Even during Gandhi's period of leadership, after every such murder there was discussion in the Congress, and usually a resolution was passed which deplored the use of violence but at the same time lauded the perpetrator for his patriotic motive. These equivocal pronouncements show that even in the years of Gandhi's leadership violence had not been repudiated by most Congressmen on moral grounds but lay just under the surface of the revolutionary movement. On many occasions when Gandhi's nonviolent campaign seemed futile, Congressmen pressed for the use of violence.

Gandhi's method of nonviolent action to produce change was not the same as passive resistance, which it was often called in the West. He himself repudiated the latter term. Those using his method were not merely to be resisting some evil; they must be striving for some positive constructive end. And they were not just to submit and suffer; this would have been negative. Rather, they were to take positive action against their injurers. The action, however, was to be without the use of violent physical force, and was to employ only force of the spirit. In extreme circumstances they could abandon mere persuasion and employ strike, cessation of business activity, non-cooperation, civil disobedience. The method was an outgrowth of Gandhi's own philosophy, and was a fusion of ideas derived from various sources, Tolstoy, Jesus in the Sermon on the Mount, and above all certain tenets of Hinduism. . . .

The conduct of the struggle was to be fundamentally in the hand of God. The method is one for the weak who are being oppressed by the strong.

Only when he has come to the extreme point of weakness and finds utter darkness all around him, only then God comes to the rescue. God helps, when a man feels humbler than the very dust under his feet. Only to the weak and helpless is the divine succor vouchsafed.

To Gandhi and his followers, the important elements in practicing *satyagraha* were the following: faith in God, a just cause, helplessness, a pure and humble heart. The leaders of such a campaign must begin by purifying themselves. Their intention must be single; they must "adopt poverty, follow truth, cultivate fearlessness"; they "have to observe perfect chastity," and besides denying sex must abstain from all other pleasures of the flesh; they may, perhaps, fast. None of their energy is to be dissipated in ends other than the main one. When the leaders are prepared, the community must observe the same vows and take a solemn oath not to submit to the injustice against which they are protesting; rather they must endure all penalties for refusal. They must, however, bear no hatred against the legislators, the police, the jailers, who oppress them. They must fill their hearts with warm love for these opponents. In the struggle they will suffer; let them be glad to do so. The suffering purifies their own souls, and at the same time becomes a force which mystically operates to their advantage, softening the hearts of their oppressors. With their love, too, they suffuse their opponents until at last a counter-love is generated in the once hard hearts. And they must ever be ready to modify their demands when reason is shown for doing so; they must be open to the arguments advanced by the other side. If the community endures unflinchingly, it must eventually triumph. But it triumphs, not by humiliating the opponents, but by bringing to them such a love that they will see that their own happiness as well as that of the community exercising soul force is best served by granting justice. They will be converted. The solution, in theory, will come as a free and joyous gift, dictated by reason and love. Thus Truth shall conquer.

That many of Gandhi's associates never believed in this method with the conviction that was Gandhi's is certain. Some openly opposed it and asked for measures of violence. Some others frankly admitted that they adhered to nonviolence only because they lacked arms. Many political leaders regarded satyagraha not as a means of practicing religion but as an opportune way of getting a mass of people to act in disciplined unity for a political end. They had no faith in mystical direction by God and the attainment of victory through the inherent power of Truth. Many, too, among the masses whom Gandhi persuaded to use satyagraha did so from opportunism rather than conviction. The bloody wholesale killings at the time of partition showed this and were the great disillusionment of Gandhi's life. To the end he preached satyagraha, but in those last months in Delhi, when with hardly intelligible words he spoke his thoughts in his evening prayer-meetings, the old fire and confidence seemed to be gone.

The opportunists, however, were not the only ones who marched behind Gandhi. There were close associates who did share his philosophy, and so did, in a simple way, many of the uneducated masses. For his method drew from an ancient and honored metaphysic in India that concerns the very nature of truth. In the Rig Veda Truth is identical with the cosmic order, and whatever conforms to it is right and belongs to the created and organized universe, while anything violating it is Untruth and is of the region of chaos where demons dwell. Every creature, man or god, has in Vedic thought his function in the universe, and for him Truth consists in fulfilling that function. . . .

Another element in Gandhi's satyagraha that had analogues in ancient India was persistence in enduring suffering for the sake of righteousness. This means not merely to undergo asceticism for achieving spiritual perfection. That feature did indeed enter in. But there was also submission to injury from one's opponent or the infliction of self-injury in his name that is a part of satyagraha and is also of ancient status in India. There is a custom in India known as "sitting dharna," that is, of sitting in obstruction before the housedoor of one who has injured you. This especially includes fasting, which may be continued unto death if the grievance is not redressed. Frequently, of course, such fasting is only a hunger strike and would not qualify as satyagraha; rather it is stubborn or malicious persistence (duragraha). The custom of threatening suicide by starvation or some other means to obtain a just demand is a powerful weapon, with a peculiar efficacy lying in the belief that if the faster should die, his death would be a sin, punishable by Heaven, charged to the account of the person against whom the fast was directed.

When Gandhi entered upon his fasts for social and political ends he was utilizing this powerful means of coercion. His opponents must in many cases have feared the consequences upon their own otherworldly future. But whether they did or not, the Hindu public saw in the fast an affirmation of just purpose, certified by Gandhi's willingness to starve to death if necessary, and a corresponding presumptive evil on the part of the opposition. If Gandhi had died in one of his fasts, those against whom the fast was directed would probably have been ruined both politically and socially. In the theory of satyagraha there is an added element, also abundantly attested in Indian legend, which translated Gandhi's practice from the level of sitting dharna to a higher sphere. This is the idea that disinterested love for an antagonist, persisting in the face of fierce assault, will accomplish conversion.

In satyagraha Gandhi adapted these various long-established notions to use by a group. This was a contribution of genius. With the use of *satyagraha* planned by capable leaders and directed in action by trained lieutenants called "volunteers," Gandhi transformed nationalist political protest from a middle-class agitation to a mass movement. Though the agricultural and industrial masses had little if any comprehension of the political or moral ends involved, they supported the campaign because of its religious content and the hope of remedying immediately and concretely their present economic distress. They were induced in consequence to make a political alliance with the professional and business bourgeoisie.

*   *   *

Gandhi's method of resistance obviously put mysticism into the nationalist struggle. To him British rule was wrong, as was the rule of any people over another; it was, in his word, "satanic." Whatever may have been the constitutional and economic issues of imperialism, they were in his eyes less than this issue of religion. But further, from the viewpoint of nationalism struggling against imperialism, his method was justified. It won mass support, when no other method had been able to do so, and by doing so contributed materially to final success. It also contributed to the peacefulness with which the transfer of power finally took place in 1947. The relative lack of violence on the nationalist side, joined with the normal British tendency to avoid extremes, let reason operate more generally than could have been foreseen in 1922, 1932, or even in 1942.

In his own major purpose Gandhi may be considered to have failed. His aim was the religious regeneration of India and Indians. As success for nationalism became step by step more likely, the politicians slipped out more and more from his control. They had no faith in the ultimate value of his religious purpose, as he had none in the ultimate worth of any purely secular end. He had said that he made a religious use of politics; many a politician of the time, if frank, would have admitted that he, in his turn, was making a political use of religion. Gandhi's own principle of nonviolence appeared to go finally into the political discard at the same time as did India's political subservience to Britain. He is venerated today by word wherever the voice of the politician is heard in the land; the wearing of homespun *khaddar* which he advocated is the mark of the Congressman holding or seeking public office; but his own dearest principle lies rusty and neglected in the political armory.

Even more, though Gandhi abhorred Hindu-Muslim communalism and partition, he nevertheless contributed to them. He could not in his time have become the political leader of the majority group in India, fortified by mass support, without being religious, he could not be religious without being Hindu. He could not be Hindu without being suspect to the Muslim community. . . .

Gandhi's economic preachings were palliative, not curative. The future building-up of India is not possible merely in his terms of village cottage industry, home spinning and weaving, land gift. Industrial expansion he viewed unsympathetically. Nor did he understand the relation of labor's troubles to national well-being. His message was one from the past, an ancient and great India reasserting itself. Once independence was won, some other leader with a different outlook, a philosophy of modernism, was needed to direct India's life in the middle of the twentieth century, and India had him at hand in Nehru.

Gandhi's Legacy to India

K. M. PANIKKAR

This final selection, from K. M. Panikkar, *The Foundations of New India* (1963), evaluates the contributions which Gandhi made to the awakening of the Indian masses, and attempts an assessment of the degree to which Gandhi's influence has a continuing significance in the India of today. Panikkar (1895–1963), a prolific historian who served his country in major diplomatic posts in China and France in the years following independence, is also the author of *Asia and Western Dominance: A Survey of the Vasco da Gama Epoch of Asian History, 1498–1945* (1959) as well as many other books.

I n the period of discontent and political frustration that followed the first Great War, Gandhiji who had by this time come to be accepted as a Mahatma — or a great soul — announced his new program for the immediate attainment of self-government of India. It was a curious jumble of many items, but its import was clear. It was a call to young India to cast aside all that it had so far cherished as essential for progress. . . . Lawyers were to give up their practice, students to turn their backs on colleges and institutions maintained or supported by government, the public to withdraw their cooperation from government and generally to organize themselves in villages and towns to live a life independent of British administration. Pressure on government was to be exercised by a program of civil disobedience, by the boycott of foreign cloth and refusal to pay taxes when the masses were organized and ready for it.

To this comprehensive policy was added a scheme known as "constructive work," the object of which was to rehabilitate the villages. The main items of this program were communal unity, removal of untouchability, prohibition of alcoholic drinks, the popularization of *khadi* or handspun cloth, village sanitation, new education, the rejection of *purdah* or the seclusion of women and the organization of peasant labour.

The older leadership, wedded to the doctrine of liberalism, saw in this movement a danger to everything it held sacred. Gandhiji was going back on Westernization: he was preaching civil disobedience of laws. He did not want young men to be educated in English. Clearly, in the view of the moderates, it was the type of reactionary leadership which was likely to undo the work of a century. But the country thought otherwise. From one end of India to the other, the common people were fired by an enthusiasm which the colourless creed of gradualism had failed to evoke. The masses had become revolutionary, for Gandhiji, not satisfied with providing a program, went from village to village all over India rousing the masses to action.

The attraction of Gandhiji's movement lay in the fact that essentially it was an appeal directed not to the psychology of the new urban classes but to that of the peasant population in India's 700,000 villages. To the masses in the villages English education of the new schools and colleges meant little or nothing and the legal theories of the liberals seemed totally unreal.

From K. M. Panikkar, *The Foundations of New India* (London, 1963), pp. 99–111, 180–188. By permission of George Allen & Unwin, Ltd.

Gandhiji devised his program in such a way as to combine into one single scheme the hope and ambitions of the villager, to give him a new zest for living, providing at the same time for such essential reforms as would purge village society of its evils. He added to the demand for independence the vision of a peasant who translates that independence into something in terms of his own immediate surroundings. . . .

All his political doctrine was colored by his vision of India as an integration of rehabilitated villages. This is what he himself has stated:

The constructive programme is the truthful and non-violent way of winning *Purna Swaraj* (independence). Its wholesale fulfilment *is* complete independence. Imagine all the forty *crores* [400 million] of people busying themselves with the whole of the constructive programme which is designed to build up the nation from the very bottom upward. Can anybody dispute the proposition that it must mean complete independence in every sense of the expression, including the ousting of foreign domination?

It is easy to see why the urban middle classes scoffed at this humdrum program, which had none of the appeal of a revolutionary political movement. Yet the masses of India recognized the message. Gandhiji was willing and quite happy to neglect the politically-minded classes for, as he expressed it, there existed "a deep chasm" between them and the masses. The politically-minded classes, by and large, rejected the new message. The Congress that accepted Gandhiji's leadership was not the same institution that a succession of very distinguished men, from W. C. Bonerji who presided at its first meeting to Lajpat Rai who presided over the special session which accepted the Gandhian doctrine, had with patient care built up and cherished for thirty-five years. To them, trained to think in terms of parliamentary procedure and to measure progress by discussion and moral persuasion, both the method of direct action which Gandhiji advocated and the reconstruction of rural life which he

conceived as the basis of India's independence were dangerously reactionary. To them *khadi* meant no more than coarse cloth, and their economics revolted against Gandhiji's ideal of going back to handspinning when obviously the future lay in industrialization. To them Gandhiji's reply was simple.

Khadi must be taken with all its implications. It means a wholesale *Swadeshi* (of one's own country) mentality, a determination to find all the necessaries of life in India and *that through the labor and intellect* of the villagers. This means a reversal of the existing process. That is to say, that instead of a half-a-dozen cities of India and Great Britain living on the exploitation and the ruin of 700,000 villages of India, the latter will be self-contained. . . . This needs a revolutionary change in the mentality and tastes of many. . . . It vitally touches the life of every single Indian, makes him feel aglow with the possession of a power that has lain hidden within himself, and makes him proud of his identity with every drop of the ocean of Indian humanity, of its economic freedom and equality and therefore ultimately, in the poetic expression of Jawaharlal Nehru, "the livery of India's freedom."

It is this identification with the humblest which made Gandhiji take up his residence in villages, to dress in a loincloth like the lowest laborer, and to live in Untouchable colonies and houses during his visits to towns. It was his principle that all the Congress workers should so far as possible be so identified. Except during periods of active political struggle, the Congress workers were expected to live in rural areas and carry on the constructive program. And in fact, whatever their limitations, the army of *khadi*-clad workers who devoted their lives to the betterment of Indian villages, carried on their labor of love among Untouchables and fallen women, introduced into the villages new ideas of sanitation, fought social prejudices and transformed the outlook of the masses in India to a greater extent during a period of twenty-five years than anything else during India's long history.

Naturally the Gandhian movement helped to alter fundamentally the traditional class relationships in India. The leadership of the non-cooperation was undoubtedly in the hands of urban classes. The many thousands of young men and women who marched in and out of jail and underwent unheard-of privations during a period of twenty-five years came mostly from the urban areas. It is they who sacrificed their all, gave up their studies in colleges and schools, broke the hearts of their parents and followed the hard path that the Mahatma laid down.

But there was a basic difference between them and the classes that provided the leadership in the earlier periods. The political classes of the past represented a prosperous middle class, men who had made their mark and were accepted in their own circles as leaders of society. The followers of the Gandhian movement were in the main young men and women who saw the vision of a free India and were moved by a spirit of service, for what Gandhiji asked them to do was to go into the villages and not merely preach the gospel of the new life, but *prove* it *by* their life work.

Those of the elder generation who followed him, prosperous lawyers like Motilal Nehru, C. R. Das and Rajagopalachari, had to sacrifice their all and adopt the strange new life which the Mahatma imposed on all his followers as the symbol not only of their sacrifice but of their identification with the peasants of the countryside. "The first thing," he insisted, "is to cultivate the mental attitude that we will not have possessions or facilities denied to millions, and the next immediate thing is to rearrange our lives as fast as possible in accordance with that mentality." The charge that Gandhiji laid on workers whom he sent to the villages may be stated in his own words as follows:

Our contact with them begins through their service, through the spinning wheel, but it does not end there. The spinning wheel is the center of that service. You will find the people cheerless and fear-stricken. You will find houses in ruins. You will look in vain for any sanitary or hygienic conditions. You will find the cattle in a miserable way and yet you will see idleness stalking there. The people will tell you of the spinning wheel having been in their homes long ago, but today they will entertain no talk of it or of any other cottage industry. They can have no scope left in them. They live, for they cannot die at will. They will spin only if you spin. Even if 100 out of a population of 300 in a village spin, you assure them of an additional income. . . . "I am alone, how can I reach 700,000 villages." This is the argument that pride whispers to us.

With an army of young men and women indoctrinated in these ideals, and distributed from one end of the country to the other, and with a program which even the illiterate peasant had no difficulty to grasp and understand, and which directly appealed to his interests and with the hope of a new age which the Mahatma was able to arouse in all, the entire atmosphere of India was changed and became charged with revolutionary tension. Gandhiji's own crusading zeal against social injustice, against the misery of the widows and the disabilities of the Untouchables, his intense faith in God and the belief in moral values, and the halo which his saintly and pure life cast on all his doings, helped by an almost superhuman energy which never tired of explaining in the minutest detail every question put to him, enabled him to convey to the vast masses a new sense of dignity, independence and self-reliance, which stood firm against all disappointments and resisted silently, but with determination, the terror, the blandishments and the bribes of the British government for over a quarter of a century.

It is the masses that stood by the *Mahatma* in his successive struggles, each one of which was followed by a wave of repression more deadly than that which preceded it.

The awakening of the masses and the shift of political emphasis from the towns to the rural areas are matters of permanent importance in the social structure of new India. The crucial problem now was to bridge the gap between the villages and the towns which an alien system of education and a mercantile economy inherited from the East India Company had forced on India. Gandhiji himself realized this and the new educational scheme which he devised and which now forms the basis of India's educational policy is an attempt to solve this question and create a basic harmony between the educated classes and the villagers. . . .

Gandhiji had a clear vision of the social purpose behind his scheme of education. "My plan," he said, "to impart primary education through the village handicrafts like spinning and carding, is thus conceived as the spearhead of a silent social revolution fraught with the most far-reaching consequences. It will provide a healthy and moral basis for relationship between the city and the village, and thus go a long way towards eradicating some of the worst evils of the present social insecurity and poisoned relationship between the classes. It will check the progressive decay of our villages and lay the foundation of a juster social order, in which there is no unnatural division between the 'haves' and 'have-nots' and everybody is assured of a living wage and the right to freedom."

*   *   *

The most far-reaching result of the Gandhian awakening of the masses has been the enlargement of the conception of democracy. The limited social classes that the earlier nationalist movement represented thought of democracy as a government by the élite. It was based on the doctrine, as Ramesh Chandra Mitra had explained, of the educated classes being the trustees of the masses, of "those who think governing those who toil." The non-cooperation movement, by basing itself on the activity of the masses and by concentrating itself on work in the rural areas, made the new nationalism an upsurge of the people and thus enlarged the conception of democracy. Gandhiji's view of politics was from the angle of the poor and exploited peasant, dependent on an uncertain monsoon, sunk in ignorance and perpetually in the clutches of the moneylender.

Though his own solution was therefore essentially a rural democracy which turned its back on large-scale industrialization, which New India under the compulsion of circumstances was forced to abandon, she has held firmly to the basic conception of a democracy in which political power is shared by all and is not confined to the modernized upper strata. The Constitution of independent India not only provides for adult suffrage with complete equality for men and women — constituting thereby by far the largest electorate in the world — but also ensures adequate representation for the depressed classes. "The real swaraj is the swaraj of the masses," Gandhiji had proclaimed. But it took a quarter of a century of struggle to transform the traditionally dumb masses of India into a vitally revolutionary force.

Thus it will be seen that the liberal political creed of Indian Nationalism was the work of the new middle classes whose rise was the most significant phenomenon in Indian social life before the Gandhian movement. This middle class created the National Congress, gave expression to the political ambitions of the educated sections of the community, developed a press and public opinion in India and provided leadership for the social reform movement which grew up side by side with nationalism. Their gradual eclipse during the Gandhian movement was not immediately noticed as the most prominent leaders of the non-cooperation movement, C. R. Das, Motilal Nehru, Abul Kalam Azad, Rajendra Prasad, Vallabhbhai Patel and others, came from these classes. But below the surface a great change was taking place. The younger leaders were not lawyers or generally men trained to liberal professions. Political activity had to spread to other classes than those from which the Congress in its earlier days recruited its members. So long as the power remained with the British this change in the class structure of the national movement did not become obvious. But with independence the situation began to change. Though national leadership continued to be in the hands of the great personalities surviving from the great struggle, Jawaharlal Nehru, Rajendra Prasad, Maulana Azad, B. C. Roy, and others, the composition of the legislatures began to show a marked change. Two tendencies were visible. The first was a shift of membership from urban to rural classes. In the past, even for rural and district constituencies, the preference was for candidates from the cities. With adult franchise and the awakening of the masses, rural interests began to assert themselves. Today in all the state legislatures there is a sizeable block of representatives from rural areas. The second noticeable shift relates to the social classes. The old middle classes represented by university men, lawyers and other professional groups have begun to yield leadership in the states to classes which had so long been denied power. The Chief Minister of one of the provinces in the period before the general election of 1962 belonged to a scheduled caste (formerly Untouchable), while the leadership in another has been in the hands of communities which though not untouchable have been considered as belonging to the lower classes. The rise of groups like the Jharkhand Party — representing aboriginal tribes — tells the same tale.

The processes of democracy have thus continued effectively the work of Mahatma Gandhi and the non-cooperation movement in awakening the masses and shifting the power from the middle classes to the common people. This is the great social integration now taking place in India, bringing to the forefront through education, use of political power and better distribution of wealth, the masses who at all times in the past have been like dumb driven cattle. The calling forth of the untapped human wealth of India, in its economic, social and intellectual urges — this indeed is the great revolution that is now taking place. The new classes emerging from below represent New India more than even the middle classes of the past whose role in intellectual leadership, in science and technology will

no doubt continue to be important, while they will be forced to yield political power to those who wield the vote.

* * *

The most spectacular and in many ways the most fundamental social change that the Gandhian movement effected in India is in respect of the position of women.

It would be wrong historically to consider that the great part that the women of India played in the non-cooperation movement and the position they have achieved for themselves in modern Indian life was the result of a sudden transformation. For over a century the process had been at work. In 1822 Ram Mohan Roy in his book entitled *Brief Remarks Regarding Modern Encroachment on the Ancient Rights of Females* had drawn attention to this problem, and had tried to prove that the condition of Hindu women in his day, when in many parts of India they were subjected to many cruel social customs, was not in keeping with the liberal teachings of early Hinduism.

* * *

From the first days of his movement Gandhiji realized that there was a source of immense untapped power in the womanhood of India which could most advantageously be turned to the work he had nearest to his heart — the rehabilitation of the villages. His appeal was addressed directly to women. Originally he seems to have been uncertain of the response, or at least of the kind of work that women could do in the national movement, for though he was a passionate believer in the equality of women, he seems to have been doubtful whether the women of India who had for so long a time been shut up in seclusion could shoulder the active leadership of a movement which called for so much physical suffering.

But when the movement was actually started, women were everywhere at the forefront. In picketing liquor shops, in enforcing the boycott of foreign cloth, and in undertaking civil disobedience they shamed men in such a way that Gandhiji continually spoke of them as the main support of his movement. There were many prominent women associated with the movement everywhere, in villages and in towns. Women all over India came forward, defying all social taboos, sacrificing physical comforts, and denying the validity of all restrictions which had been enforced against them, to take up every kind of work connected with the national movement.

They were from all classes — from Sarojini Naidu, poet, social reformer, President of the Congress, to humble women of the Untouchables, princesses like Rajkumari Amrit Kaur and wives of millionaires to the commonest village folk. And strange was the fact that the wives of many loyal officials working in all earnestness and sincerity on the side of the British Government were brave enough openly to take up the constructive side of the movement. . . .

Equal participation of women in the struggle thus became the motto of *satyagraha* and this spirit of active interest in public life grew with the prolongation of the movement for over twenty-five years. If the first movement of 1921 had succeeded and *swaraj* had then been won, the awakening of Indian women would have only been superficial. It is the hardening effect of the continuing revolution and generation after generation of women growing up in an atmosphere not only of tension but calling for every sacrifice that gave women their present place in Indian life. There was no suffragette movement in India, no feminism, for the share of women in the battle of freedom gave them their position of equality without their having to fight for it separately. It was a matter of surprise to the outside world that independent India should have appointed women to the highest posts so freely, as members of the Cabinet, as governors of Provinces, as ambassadors and as leaders of delegations to international conferences, for *ex hypothesi* in an Oriental country such as India, women are presumed to be held in

subjection and therefore all this seemed to be unnatural. What caused even greater surprise was that these women, hardened by many terms in jail, should have been not merely ornamental figures but able in every sense to hold their own with the ablest of any country.

It is not the distinction achieved by a few women of genius that is the true test of the changed position of women in India. What really is epochal and marks a revolutionary change is their free and equal participation in all spheres of national activity, and at every level, from work in villages to the government of the country. It was never a part of the Indian tradition that women were by nature inferior: on the contrary the ancient tradition emphasized their equality, though later social disabilities rendered it impossible for women to exercise that equality or to participate in many fields of activity. What the Gandhian movement did was to release women from the social bondages that custom had imposed and conservatism had upheld.

*   *   *

The question remains and is often asked whether in the political life of India today, after fifteen years of independence, the Mahatma exercises any considerable influence; whether such influence as he still exercises is not a diminishing one, and whether, when those who were immediately associated with him, an aging group who in the course of the next few years are bound gradually to disappear, cease to guide Indian politics, anything will be left of Gandhism.

To a casual observer, the achievements of India after independence would appear to be based on other than Gandhian principles. It is not on the basis of handicraft industry, as Gandhiji hoped and Gandhian economics taught, that India has during the last fifteen years built up her economy. Her giant steel mills and other enterprises in the public sector represent the very opposite of Gandhian teaching. In fact, the so-called Gandhian economists in India denounce them as a betrayal. Rapid large-scale industrialization is the ideal that India has set for herself. That it is different from Gandhiji's vision of India requires no proof for his whole life was a protest against industrialized society.

To him *khaddar* or *khadi* represented an ideal of civilization, a symbol of human necessities being satisfied by men and women individually working in villages. True, most Congress leaders even now wear *khadi*; on formal occasions such as Gandhiji's birthday they even spin. The Central and local governments also give considerable financial and other support for the production and sale of *khadi*. But for all this demonstrative allegiance to the Mahatma's doctrines, very few will today claim for his teachings any influence on India's policy. We no longer hear of *ahimsa* or nonviolence — a principle to which Gandhi attached fundamental importance. On the other hand, India is straining every nerve to arm herself to the teeth. That every nation requires armed forces for its defense — however much Mr. Khrushchev may talk of total disarmament — is obvious. Not even during Gandhiji's lifetime did the Congress leaders in India accept the doctrine of nonviolence in regard to defense. But India's policy has gone much beyond the doctrine of essential self-defense. No doubt this is due to the growth of conditions on her borders which compelled India to interpret the requirements of her defense rather elastically. . . .

The same oblivion has not fallen on the Mahatma's doctrine of *satyagraha* as an effective weapon in politics only because minor political leaders here and there show a tendency to degrade it by invoking its name to cover every kind of ridiculous agitation. But the failure of these so-called *satyagrahas* has only helped to discredit what was in the hands of the Mahatma an irresistible instrument of mass action. With free political institutions functioning at all levels, from the central government to village *panchayats*,[1] with freedom of speech,

and full civil liberties, it becomes difficult to wield *satyagraha* as a political weapon on a national scale. To use it for limited local purposes has been found to be ineffective when other and more effective courses of action are open to the public.

If *satyagraha,* as Gandhiji viewed it, has disappeared from the political scene, fasting as a political weapon, which also was one of the Gandhian techniques, today stands totally discredited. The Mahatma resorted to this weapon only when he considered moral issues were at stake. But fasting by political leaders in the post-independence period has been mainly to secure some political point which had no moral issues behind it. . . .

Another aspect of Gandhian thought was the Mahatma's distrust of state action. It was one of his sayings that he liked that government which governed the least. His idea of a state was that of an individualist who considered state action, outside a limited sphere, to be interference with the individual's liberties. He was in fact a determined opponent of the leviathan state. In this sphere also he could not be said to have influenced Indian thinking. The major characteristic of India's development after independence is the growth of state functions in all directions. Economic planning, social legislation, community development, educational policies — in fact in every sphere of human interest — the new Indian State has extended its activities. It has even tried to organize the *sadhus, sanyasis* [holy men, religious ascetics] who have renounced the world. Nowhere has the departure from the Gandhian ideal been so great as in the development of state activities. Indian politics are libertarian but the Indian State is totalitarian only as a welfare state can be.

In what may be called minor issues also, Gandhian ideals have come under eclipse. Prohibition was an idea very dear to the Mahatma. In his lifetime the elimination of alcoholic drinks was an important plank in all Congress programs. So deeply was

---

[1] The *panchayat* was the village council in traditional Indian society. *Panchayati raj* is the term given to the system of rural self-government which has been developed in India since independence. [Editor's note]

the Congress committed to this policy that its impetus continued for a time even after India became independent. But what is the position now? Though Congressmen as a body claim to be teetotalers, prohibition as a national policy is not even being talked about. With some difficulty the States in which prohibition was introduced in the first enthusiasm are carrying on with it even now. There is however no talk now of enforcing it on an all-India scale.

If *ahimsa* and *satyagraha* are not doctrines which exercise any great influence in Indian politics, if *khadi* economics and handicraft civilization have been discarded in favour of large-scale industrialization based on continuous planning and state control, if India is developing into a welfare state with planned activities extending to every sphere, what then is left of the Mahatma's inheritance? It is obvious that India is now developing along lines which the Mahatma had opposed during his entire lifetime. This cannot be denied. In fact the true-blue Gandhians in India from Vinoba Bhave and Mira Ben down to the least important occupants of *ashrams* in different parts of India openly complain that Gandhiji has been betrayed and that the India that is developing before their eyes is something which would have appeared monstrous to Gandhiji's eyes. Would it then be right to say that the Mahatma is now no more than a legend to which people pay homage and that his teachings have no more influence with the people of India? That would indeed be an exaggeration. Though his economic ideas have been discarded — and in fact would never seem to have been seriously accepted or believed in — and his political methods are no longer considered useful or effective, there are important spheres of national life where the Mahatma's teachings continue to shape national policy. The most important of these is the burning sense of social justice which he brought into national life, and which showed itself most prominently in his identification with the *Harijans* in India. Nothing moved him so much as the inhumanity with which Hin-

duism had throughout history treated the Depressed Classes. To him untouchability was the great sin for which India was paying the penalty. His approach to this question was not of a social reformer but of a humble penitent who identified himself with the oppressed. He lived by preference in *Harijan* colonies. He was prepared to sacrifice everything, even his life, to safeguard their interests. This passionate revolt against a crying injustice was perhaps the most important aspect of his political life and some of it he has been able to transmit not only to his followers but to the people of India as a whole.

The sense of social injustice which is one of the characteristics of new India is undoubtedly a part of what India has inherited from Gandhiji. If Untouchability has been abolished and its practice in any form made a penal offense, if the so-called Untouchables of yesterday share effective political power both in the Center and in the States, if special provision is made for their educational, economic and social advancement, it is undoubtedly due to the great impetus that the Mahatma gave to the sense of social justice as a basis for national life.

Again, India's emphasis on the village and on what has been called *panchayati raj* is a part of the inheritance of Gandhiji. All his life Gandhiji had insisted that real *swaraj* can only be *swaraj* for the villages. Cities were anathema to him. He considered urban life as representing something evil. In an interview with foreign correspondents at Mussoorie in 1946 Gandhiji declared:

I consider the growth of cities to be an evil thing, unfortunate for mankind and the world . . . and certainly unfortunate for India. The British have exploited India through its cities. The latter have exploited the villages. The blood of the villages is the cement with which the edifice of the cities is built. I want the blood that is today inflating the arteries of the cities to run once again in the blood vessels of the villages. . . .

While it is undeniably true that India's great and fundamental reform of *panchayati raj* can be directly traced to this teaching of the Mahatma and is perhaps the most abiding of all the lessons that she has learnt from him, the very significant differences between what India has adopted and what he taught are illustrative of the character of Gandhiji's influence. India has rejected totally and utterly Gandhiji's objection to the growth of cities. In fact the period of India's independence has witnessed the planning and development of many cities, especially around industrial complexes. Chittaranjan, Durgapur, Bhilai, Rourkela are but a few of the more outstanding examples. Great ports like Kandla have been built up from marshes. Townships like Nilokheri and Faridabad have been created to accommodate refugees from Pakistan. New capital cities, Chandigarh and Bhubaneswar, have come into being. Within twelve years the population of Delhi has jumped from a mere 700,000 to 2,500,000. Many satellite towns have grown up around the older cities. In fact all over India this development of cities and townships is going on and the government far from discouraging it, as it should do according to Gandhian principles, is actively encouraging the movement. The government believes that in India the percentage of rural population is higher than it should be and a deliberate effort is therefore being made to absorb them in urban industries. While emphasizing the value of small industrial units based on villages, the government also holds that the economic development of India will never be satisfactory unless it is based on modern large-scale industries which have to be grouped around towns or which would inevitably develop townships around them. Consequently the basic assumption of the Mahatma that cities are the handiwork of the devil and are "evil" is decisively rejected by New India.

Even in respect of village organization, Indian leadership does not follow Gandhiji the whole way. Nehru has accepted from the Mahatma the doctrine of the village as the base on which to build the political democracy of India. But his *panchayati raj*, while giving to the village an effective voice in many important aspects of village life, integrates it with higher organizations. With Gandhiji the village is an independent unit. . . . Gandhiji's idea of each village "being a complete republic" finds no support in the policies of New India but they have accepted and given shape to his essential doctrine that real India lives in the villages and that India's freedom, if it is to mean anything substantial, must not only mean a better life for the people of the villages, but a life which they will be allowed to shape themselves. This indeed is the living part of Gandhiji's teaching that the predominantly urban leadership which took over from him has not forgotten. It is no mere lip-service they pay to this doctrine, as in the case of *khadi* and handicrafts, but a genuine effort to translate it into practice so that India will not be merely a formal democracy, but essentially one in which the millions in the villages will be effective participants.

India's approach to private wealth may also be said in a measure to be an inheritance from Gandhiji. No doubt it has much earlier roots. At no time did India consider wealth to be the measure of value; nor did a man receive honour or exercise power in terms of his wealth. It was perhaps one of the few good results of the caste conception that the money-maker or *Vaisya* came only after the *Brahmin* and the *Kshatriya*. No doubt the worship of wealth and the political importance of money are results of an industrial society, for even in feudal Europe wealth as such counted for little as against status. In India the persistence of caste gradation added to this tendency. But with the transition to an industrial society the danger was no doubt there of the new capitalist classes getting control of the machinery of government and utilizing it for their benefit. It was generally insinuated in anti-Indian circles — indeed at one time it became a part of British propaganda — that since a few millionaires were included in the Mahatma's circle and he at times used to stay with them, that the Congress under his leadership had become the instrument of the capitalist classes. There was never any danger of this. From the beginning the Mahatma identified himself with the *daridra narayan* (God as a poor man) — was the champion of the poor and the dispossessed. He was never impressed by wealth, nor was he willing at any time to accept the idea that wealth conferred any privilege. Speaking at the London Round Table Conference in 1931 he defined his attitude to special interests as follows:

Above all the Congress represents in its essence the dumb semi-starved millions scattered over the length and breadth of the land. Every interest which in the opinion of the Congress is worthy of protection has to subserve the interests of these dumb millions: and so you will find again and again apparently a clash between several interests, and if there is a genuine clash, I have no hesitation in saying, on behalf of the Congress, that the Congress will sacrifice every interest for the sake of the interest of these dumb millions.

This was an unequivocal dedication on a formal occasion before the representatives of all sections of opinion both in India and in Britain. And it was a clear warning that vested interests whether British or Indian would not receive any consideration at his hands when they came into conflict with the interests of the poor. This emphasis on the overriding interests of the masses and the determination to make all other interests subserve the masses is one of the most valuable things inherited by modern India from Gandhiji's teaching.

Independent India has made no secret of the fact that its policy as far as possible is to eliminate glaring inequalities in wealth, and to use for this purpose the entire power of state machinery — through heavier and often differentiating taxation on the rich, through exclusion of private interests from many important spheres of economic activity, by abolishing zamindaries and other forms of landlordism, by placing a ceiling on landholdings, etc. This policy no doubt has a twofold origin, from the Mahatma as

well as from Marx. While undoubtedly the influence of socialist thinking is a major factor in the shaping of India's economic policy . . . this idea of levelling economic differences and of considering the wealthy as a sinister interest whose claims to importance and influence should be watched and controlled is undoubtedly a part of Gandhian teaching which has taken deep root in India. Whether it would have been as effective as it has proved to be without the economic and social urges provided by socialism is something which requires examination.

Briefly, it may be said that some of the teachings of Gandhiji have passed into the general traditions of India, but strangely enough not those to which he attached the greatest importance, *ahimsa, satyagraha,* voluntary poverty, etc. Indeed, in the case of the importance he attached to villages as the basis of national life, India has rejected certain essential aspects of his approach to the problem, as for example his view that villages should be republics, that cities in themselves are evil. His successors have taken over only as much of his teaching as can be accommodated in an industrial society, in which rural life would itself be urbanized to a large extent and *panchayats,* while entrusted with wide powers, would be integrated with national life. What India has inherited from Gandhiji is thus important and is undoubtedly a continuing factor. In many cases, like social reform, betterment of women, Gandhi's influence has given only an additional impetus to an already growing movement 100 years old. In others, like the abolition of untouchability, the widening of Hinduism to include in it all the classes which had been considered *avarnas* — or outside the caste system — his teaching, practice and influence was the predominant factor. All in all, the Mahatma is justly acclaimed the Father of the Nation, though with the growth of an industrialized society, it is difficult to be certain whether his influence will continue.

SUGGESTIONS FOR ADDITIONAL READING

There are numerous biographical studies of Gandhi which will prove useful to the student. The most readily available are two books by Louis Fischer, *Gandhi: His Life and Message for the World* (New York, 1954) and *The Life of Mahatma Gandhi* (New York, 1950); both may be obtained in inexpensive paperbound editions. The most detailed account is the eight-volume work by D. G. Tendulkar, *Mahatma* (Delhi, 1960), which utilizes extensive quotations from Gandhi's own voluminous writings. The later years of Gandhi's life are similarly covered in detail in Pyarelal [Nair], *Mahatma Gandhi: The Last Phase* (2 vols., Ahmedabad, 1956). A short study by B. R. Nanda, *Mahatma Gandhi: A Biography* (London, 1958) is also worthy of mention. Gandhi's own *Autobiography: The Story of My Experiments with Truth* (Washington, 1954) only covers the period to 1921. All the works mentioned above are sympathetic in approach; indeed, critical studies of Gandhi and his impact on India are few in number compared with those which range from appreciative to adulatory. A comprehensive annotated listing of Gandhiana is given in Jagdish Saran Sharma, *Mahatma Gandhi: A Descriptive Bibliography* (Delhi, 1955).

Two paperbound collections of Gandhi's own writings are *The Essential Gandhi*, Louis Fischer, ed. (New York, 1963) and *The Gandhi Reader*, Homer Jack, ed. (New York, 1961).

The student of Gandhi's place in modern Indian history will want also to consult works on Indian nationalism, among which may be mentioned the official Congress history by B. Pattabhi Sitaramayya, *History of the Indian National Congress* (2 vols., Madras, 1935–47), presenting Gandhi in a favorable light; R. C. Majumdar, *History of the Freedom Movement in India* (3 vols., Calcutta, 1962–63), a critical work; and A. R. Desai, *Social Background of Indian Nationalism*, 3rd ed. (Bombay, 1959), which sets nationalist development in its social context. The events of the Gandhian era in Indian politics may be viewed through the eyes of Jawaharlal Nehru in his *Autobiography* (London, 1936; published in New York in 1941 as *Toward Freedom*), while Subhas Chandra Bose has told the story of the two non-cooperation movements in his *The Indian Struggle, 1920–1934* (London, 1935), a work which makes apparent the author's distaste for Gandhian methods. Maulana Abul Kalam Azad, the most important Muslim in the Congress leadership, has reviewed the events of the period from 1935 through 1947 in his *India Wins Freedom* (Bombay, 1959).

Perhaps the most effective presentation of Gandhi's *satyagraha* as a technique for social change is Krishnalal Shridharani, *War Without Violence* (New York, 1939; reprinted in a paper edition in Bombay, 1962). A similarly sympathetic approach is taken by the American political scientist, Joan V. Bondurant, in her *Conquest of Violence: The Gandhian Philosophy of Conflict* (Princeton, 1958). Indira Rothermund, *The Philosophy of Restraint: Mahatma Gandhi's Strategy of Politics* (Bombay, 1963) is a stimulating and provocative study, as is also T. K. N. Unnithan, *Gandhi and Free India: A Socio-Economic Study* (Groningen, 1956).